FISH

SEASIDE RESORTS

OLDIE PUBLICATIONS

SEASIDE RESORTS

CANDIDA LYCETT GREEN

First published in 2011
by Oldie Publications Ltd
65 Newman Street, London W1T 3EG
www.theoldie.co.uk

A catalogue record for this book
is available from the British Library

ISBN: 978-1-901170-17-7

Printed and bound in the UK by Butler Tanner & Dennis Ltd

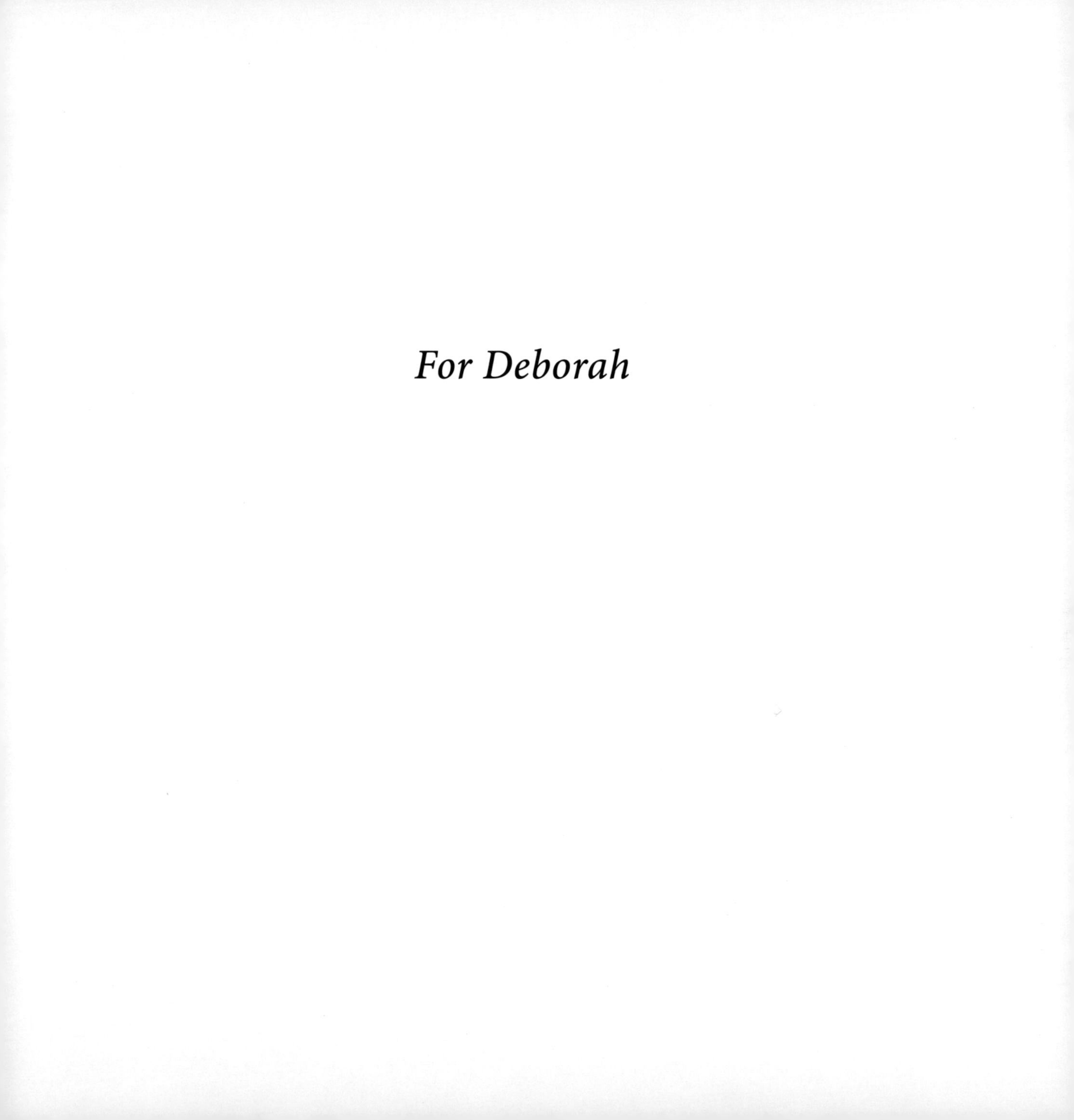

For Deborah

Contents

Introduction

The sea is part of us. As islanders, it has been our safeguard for thousands of years and, in Swinburne's words, 'we, sons and sires of seamen whose home is all the sea' are never far away from its edge. Though we now forget how the sea shaped our history, we have always had an affinity with it. There are more than eleven thousand miles of coastline around Great Britain, and because ours is the most geologically complicated country in the world, the variety is infinite. Within relatively short distances the terrain changes dramatically – from the wooded cliffs of Ventnor on the Isle of Wight, for instance, where Swinburne hymned his beloved sea, to the low-lying emptiness of dunes around Skegness, from the mountain-backed beaches of North Wales to the great shoulders of chalk downland above the Sussex coast. Developers inevitably plumped for the very best sites – often encompassing existing villages or fishing communities. On my journeys around the coast I have been amazed by the beauty of some of their natural settings: Llandudno, for instance, or Eastbourne, Scarborough, Tenby and Ilfracombe.

The first glimpse of the sea after an absence always excites me – a feeling triggered no doubt by the memory of childhood holidays; memories which we in turn pass on to our children and grandchildren. The bright and breezy nature of seaside architecture in, say, Brighton, Torquay or Sidmouth suggests uncomplicated pleasure. For me resorts are places where, when you face out to sea, your cares are behind you: the promenades and seawalls are the safe divider between the civilised world and the wild. Walking their lengths you have the best of both.

I visited almost a hundred resorts in England and Wales, mostly out of season and more often than not in the rain. My visits were as a weekending tourist or a day-tripper, not as a social analyst or academic. I had no preconceptions and judged each place as I found it. I went with the intention of enjoying myself and my first port of call was always the seafront. It was a tough test, but in all the fifty places I have chosen, I genuinely felt uplifted. That, after all, is the point of a seaside resort. Nearly all of them were purpose-built around a beach and existed to restore the spirit and to engender a sense of gaiety and freedom. The flamboyance of the architecture along the promenade, the excitement levels of the funfairs, the loveliness of the public gardens, the engineering brilliance of the piers and lifts, the encompassing cosiness

of the old harbours, and the beauty of the bays and beaches may have been persuasive factors but, combined with the ever-consoling sea, it was the *atmosphere* of each of my chosen places which swayed me the most. The spirit of enjoyment left by generations of past holidaymakers must have had something to do with it.

The rivalry I came across between neighbouring resorts was often fierce. Frinton, for instance, hardly acknowledges the existence of Walton on the Naze, even though their suburbs merge; Lytham St Anne's has always looked down on Blackpool, while many Bexhill residents will spend their whole lives without ever setting foot in St Leonard's, although it is only a mile away. Snobbery has always been rife: when our first brilliant entrepreneurs invented the seaside resort, and the cult of the seaside began to emerge in the late seventeenth century, they used exclusivity as a prime selling point.

Three hundred years ago we were in awe of the sea and did not consider it in any way beautiful; it was the necessary haunt of our sailors, not to mention smugglers and fishermen. The villages and towns on the coast lay huddled around harbours protected from the weather, and hardly any great houses were built within sight of the sea. Only relatively recently has there been a radical shift of consciousness, from a fear of the sea to a positive desire to be beside it.

One of the catalysts for this change of heart was Robert Wittie, the first 'doctor' to prescribe bathing in seawater as a curative in the late 1660s. On his advice a growing group of sickly socialites, rich enough to afford his prices, gathered to face the sea at Scarborough.

The first bathing machine was built about fifty years later, and the village expanded to accommodate the influx of visitors. The fad of the 'seaside' spread like wildfire through the eighteenth century, and a host of doctors continued to propagate the amazing healing properties of saltwater. Astute entrepreneurs, often in cahoots with the doctors, were quick to cash in on this new phenomenon. Soon the great spa towns, such as Harrogate, Tunbridge Wells, Bath and Cheltenham, began losing their hypochondriacal mineral-water-taking visitors to the seaside. Dr Richard Russell's famous *Dissertation on the Use of Sea Water*, published in 1752, was in its fourth edition by 1760, and when he

decided to build a house for himself in the little village of Brighthelmstone, hundreds of fashionable invalids followed in his wake to what is now called Brighton. By the time the Prince Regent came to town twenty years later (having been told that the sea might help his unsightly goitre), the desire for good health was already merging with pleasure-seeking. 'Watering places' saw regular gatherings of the higher echelons of society who felt reassured by the kudos of being seen in the very latest place, even though their health did not necessarily improve. After all, Margate's Dr Lettsom, who opened a Sea Bathing Infirmary in the 1790s, did not promise anything. He wrote his own epitaph, which read:

When people's ill, they comes to I;
I physics, bleeds and sweats 'em,
Sometimes they live, sometimes they die;
What's that to I? J. Lettsom.

While doctors up and down the land were promoting the sea as the perfect panacea, the Picturesque Movement was gathering momentum. Its instigators informed the would-be-cultivated that rugged natural scenery was not only beautiful, but sublime. Having turned their backs on the sea to spend their time taming nature into gardens and parks, they were now encouraged to view the terrifying wildness of the sea's edge with fresh eyes. Charlotte Brontë is said to have burst into tears when she first saw the sea. Jane Austen, on the other hand, mocked the movement's intellectual pretension. She describes Sir Edward Denham strolling along the terrace of her fictitious resort of Sanditon, extolling the sea's virtues to Charlotte Heyward: 'He began in a tone of great Taste and Feeling, to talk of the Sea and the Seashore and ran through all the usual Phrases in praise of the Sublimity, and descriptive of the undescribable emotions they excite in the Mind of Sensibility.'

By the beginning of the nineteenth century the idea of spending time beside the sea had been sold to those with money and time on their hands, and it wasn't surprising that the great seaside property boom took hold. Rather than staying in lodgings or inns as they had done in the past, the new holidaymakers could now buy or rent a villa, or a grand stucco terrace house, or stay in a newfangled 'hotel'. Aristocratic landowners, whose vast acres beside the sea had been languishing as uncommercial farmland, suddenly found themselves sitting on goldmines. Visionary new towns sprang up under their auspices with wide tree-lined boulevards and avenues bearing their names – Devonshire Place in Eastbourne, Lumley Avenue in Skegness, De La Warr Parade in Bexhill or Mostyn Avenue in Llandudno. (The beaches, however, have always belonged to the Crown, so remain by definition open to everyone.)

But it was the coming of the railways which had the greatest impact of all and opened much of the hitherto inaccessible coastline to the general public, as well as to speculative property developers. Previously, visitors travelled by passenger steamer to remote places like Ilfracombe. Now they came by rail in their thousands. By 1850 six thousand miles of track had been laid and the railway companies exploited their coastlines by offering cheap excursions. In June 1841 Skegness only had 44 visitors. The railway arrived in 1873, and on the August Bank Holiday of 1882 it brought an estimated 22,000 day-trippers, 20,000 of whom paid to go onto the newly-built pier. In one week of good weather in 1859 73,000 people travelled by train to Brighton. In *Alice in Wonderland*, Alice concluded: 'Wherever you go to on the English coast, you find a number of bathing machines in the sea, some children digging in the sand with wooden spades, then a row of lodging houses, and behind them a railway station.'

With the growth of the railways came a sense of optimism which swept the nation. Our engineering genius was at its height and there was an adventurous approach to new materials. A whole new generation of the rich middle class was there for the seducing, and resorts became a perfect display cabinet for ever more dazzling Victorian design in the form of palatial winter gardens, pavilions, fanciful balconies and bandstands, ballrooms, theatres, two-tiered promenades, elaborate ornamental pleasure gardens with miniature canals and, perhaps most innovative of all, the seaside pier, developed in the first place as a landing stage for the passenger steamers. Piers became a necessary, if sometimes purely cosmetic, feature of a successful resort – and 'pleasure' was the word which pervaded all.

From the outset our resorts were unique. We led the world. One of the first Grand Hotels opened in Scarborough in 1867 and for over a decade was the premier hotel of Europe. Nice and Monte Carlo merely copied us. The bonus of royal patronage was used mercilessly to sell resorts, and Weymouth's promoters

were among the first to boast of George III's regular visits. Sidmouth claimed the infant Queen Victoria, Cromer the Prince of Wales, and Bognor George IV, but in the end this wasn't enough to prevent the fashionable rich from choosing to holiday abroad. Anyway, many were unhappy about the type of visitor who came with the railway boom. Even democratic Dickens complained that the tone of his much-loved Broadstairs was being lowered by the presence of the hoi polloi. When Bank Holidays were created in 1871 (the brainchild of cricket-loving Liberal MP John Lubbock), day-trippers arrived in droves. Over fifty per cent of the population were by now living in grimy towns, and day trips to the seaside were not only deemed to be healthily invigorating but were synonymous with good fun. Some enlightened factory owners even paid for their workforce to go. Resorts were now no longer the exclusive haunt of the rich. They belonged to the ordinary man whose appetite for oompah bands, music hall, donkey rides, shell souvenirs, rock, dirty postcards, floral clocks and spectacular carpet bedding added still further to the general merriment of the seaside.

After the First World War various unions had negotiated paid, week-long holidays for their workers, the production of the first Austin Seven saw the birth of mass motoring, the notion of sunbathing had been born on the Riviera and the nation was beginning to fall for American culture. Billy Butlin introduced dodgem cars to Skegness and then, in 1936, built the first of his vast holiday camps there. He had noticed how English families kept themselves to themselves and often looked increasingly gloomy as their holiday wore on. His Red Coats changed all that. They took the children off their parents' hands and marshalled everyone into having a good time. It was a brilliant and radical concept at just the right moment. In 1937 an estimated fifteen million were taking annual holidays and Butlin's prices suited the lowest paid. In 1939 100,000 people visited the Butlin's camps at Skegness and Clacton.

Meanwhile, resorts were investing fortunes in keeping up with the times by building state-of-the-art lidos, like the Jubilee Pool in Penzance or the Saltdean Lido in Brighton; daring apartment blocks, like Marine Court in St Leonards; and funfairs and amusement arcades. Railway companies, who had previously used words like 'bracing' and 'breezy' to advertise holiday destinations, were now creating beautifully seductive posters which were all about sunshine. By the 1950s a fortnight's paid holiday became statutory, and for the next twenty-five years British resorts were as popular as they had ever been. Then everything changed. Cheap air travel and package holidays, coupled with the desire to deepen our tans and have access to cheap wine, meant that most of us forsook the British seaside resort, which had been part of our holiday lives for centuries.

But as Travis Elborough remarks in his beautifully observed study of the English seaside, *Wish You Were Here*, the tide has turned. Some of the resorts in this book have undergone, or are undergoing, a renaissance. The buzz that is created around the restoration of an architectural landmark, like the De La Warr Pavilion in Bexhill-on-Sea, the addition of a spectacular new art gallery or restaurant, or famous resident artists and writers, can, like Dr Wittie in Scarborough or the Prince Regent in Brighton, bring the fashionable sheep flocking. There are also several places in this book which are not resorts in the Victorian sense of the word, but which have created their own momentum. Around the early 1900s various artistic circles evolved out of the holiday crowds in a handful of undeveloped fishing villages where the light was beautiful and the rent cheap. In their wake came myriad camp followers who felt the need to rediscover the picturesque and enjoyed rubbing shoulders with the bohemian set. The latest new seaside sports were on hand: golf on the duney links, sailing around romantic creeks and inlets, and, by the 1930s, surfing. St Ives, Fowey, Salcombe, Padstow, Wells-next-the-Sea and their environs became the latest 'resorts', and remain in some cases the exclusive and exorbitantly expensive domains of today's *jeunesse dorée*, where latter-day royalty, in the form of 'celebrities', are occasionally spotted. It's the same old story.

The architecture of our resorts remains, on the whole, brilliant – if occasionally tattered. The Germans may have made holes in our South Coast promenades, planning committees may have made disastrous decisions, the approach roads through remorseless hinterlands of Asdas and roundabouts may be dispiriting, and the dream-like infinity of the sea's horizon may be compromised by wind turbines, but the terrain remains the same and the tides forever renew the landscape of their beaches. For my money, ours are still the best seaside resorts in the world.

CANDIDA LYCETT GREEN
AUGUST 2011

Aberdovey, Merionethshire

Past gloomy grey slate quarries hacked out of hillsides, sheepdogs speeding up bracken-y valleys, and one of the oldest Outward Bound schools of all, Aberdovey curls round the shoreline, modest and beautiful. Its long stucco terraces of pastel-shaded, bay-windowed bed-and-breakfasts face out across marram grass, low dunes and generous sands towards Ireland, while its more sheltered heart faces due south across the mile-wide mouth of the River Dovey to a hazy view of Borth Sands. Voluptuously wooded hills rise high and steep behind, protecting the town from the north wind. In consequence its gardens are luxurious, its winters mild, its fat hydrangeas brick pink and its *magnolia grandiflora* flowers as big as pint-sized teacups. The older houses and hostelries – the half-timbered Dovey Inn and the Penhelig Arms – line the sheltered shore-side, and behind them larger, well-to-do villas tuck into the hill.

It was the temperate climate which inveigled the Ruck family to spend three months of every year in Aberdovey, abandoning their colder home nine miles up-river. In the 1880s young Arthur Ruck, who had recently taken up golf, brought his clubs to Aberdovey. For want of a golf course he found a piece of common land where he set out nine flower pots as holes and created a course where his friends and relations, including two of Charles Darwin's sons, played with him. Aberdovey became a winter resort for a nucleus of close-knit families, and gradually the course gained a reputation. Today it ranks as one of the greatest in the world, and you can play golf here on Christmas Day in your shirt sleeves.

The Cambrian Coast railway, which crosses the spectacular Mawddach estuary from Barmouth on its long clumpy bridge and snakes on down to Aberdovey's station, is a legacy from the town's lucrative copper mining days. The line then carries on under the hill and through a black rock cutting to Penhelig's tiny station at the far end of the town. As always in Wales, God is never far away. Jammed in here and there are a Calvinistic Methodist chapel, an English Presbyterian church, a Wesleyan Methodist chapel and St Peter's parish church. I walked into Copperhill Street and found a footpath spiralling upwards between slate-grey houses and high garden walls where ivy-leaved toadflax clung to the crevices. The path led to a high grassy knoll topped by a little bandstand, sadly no longer used. The local builder, who was repairing its columns, told me, 'By the time the band got up here they were so puffed they couldn't blow their instruments.'

Right: the northern end of Aberdovey

I HEAR THOSE VOICES
THA WILL OT BE ROWNED

Aldeburgh, Suffolk

Half of Elizabethan Aldeburgh is under the sea. Walking along the colour-washed High Street, with its mock-Tudor cinema and famous Cragg Sisters tea shop, the waves sound dangerously close at hand. The old Moot Hall, which used to stand in the middle of the town, is now at the sea's edge, and the adjoining hamlet of Slaughden – to which the characters in Wilkie Collins's unsung novel *No Name* would take their walks from Aldeburgh – has disappeared, its odd remnants occasionally visible at low spring tides. A Martello Tower remains, looking as though it might be sucked into the sea, and beyond it the city of Dunwich, once a great medieval port, lies drowned in the deeps. They say its church bells have been heard ringing above the sound of the waves on wild and stormy nights. In 1848 the Rev Alfred Suckling warned the dreamer, 'lest he be misled by imaginary light. For unlike those ruined cities whose fragments attest their former grandeur, Dunwich is wasted, desolate, and void. Its palaces and temples are no more ...'

This far-flung and mysterious edge of Suffolk has long drawn an artistic crowd. The poet Crabbe was born here and his poem 'The Borough' is based on Aldeburgh. M R James, our greatest ghost story writer, whose grandparents lived at Wyndham House near the church (where his father became curate), was inspired by this eerie stretch of coast. But Aldeburgh's most famous son is Benjamin Britten who, with his partner Peter Pears, made a home here, and in 1948 founded the now celebrated music festival. (The libretto for Britten's opera *Peter Grimes* is adapted from Crabbe's poem.)

A hundred years earlier, with some success, Newson Garrett, a local brewer and maltster, began to develop Aldeburgh as a seaside resort. Elizabeth, one of Newson's six vehemently feminist daughters, became the first woman doctor in Britain against all odds and ended up as mayor of Aldeburgh in 1908. Her husband created the golf course, while her sister Millicent became president of the women's suffragette movement.

If you walk northwards along Crag Path beside the beach, past Newson Garrett's tall, gabled and occasionally wacky boarding houses, you will see Maggi Hambling's beautiful scallop shell sculpture on the low skyline ahead, her tribute to Benjamin Britten. It is set above the steep shingle shoreline with the words (from *Peter Grimes*): 'I hear those voices that will not be drowned.'

Main: Maggi Hambling's scallop shell
Inset: the town steps

Alnmouth, Northumberland

The north Northumbrian coast remains perhaps the most romantic of all. Alnmouth sits on a sandy peninsula between the melancholy castles of Dunstanburgh, towering into the grey sky from its rugged black rock headland, and Warkworth, Harry Hotspur's daunting fortress. The Dukes of Northumberland still own huge tracts of the county, as they have done for centuries, and there is a pervading air of feudalism and toughness.

Alnmouth faces away from the sea and into the sheltering crook of its beautiful river estuary. Its harbour was its fortune from neolithic times, and by the end of the eighteenth century it was a prosperous grain port which, when Wesley made a brief stop there, was 'rife with smuggling and famous for all types of wickedness'. The advent of bigger ships and the shifting of sands during a violent storm on Christmas Day in 1806 saw its gradual decline, and when the main East Coast railway line came, its trade was further hit.

The railway performed its usual magic, however, by bringing visitors. Suddenly Alnmouth, with its beautiful dune-backed beach, winding streets and picturesque granaries, became a fashionable venue for a handful of rich Victorian families from Newcastle and further afield who felt they had 'discovered' it. Fenwicks, Cadogans, Peases and Brownes converted granaries, renovated the larger existing houses or built brand-new holiday homes. They drew in a large crowd of socially aspiring followers. Public baths were installed, heated by the new gas works, and it became a fashionable pastime to stroll down Northumberland Street and gather at the estuary every evening. In 1869 Captain Arthur Walker founded one of the first golf clubs in Britain and employed the young Mungo Park (who later became famous as a golfer and course designer) as the club's first professional. In the 1920s the club leased more land from the Duke of Northumberland to build an eighteen-hole course designed by Mr H S Colt.

Today Alnmouth is a quiet and unassuming place – its brief wave of fashionable popularity having died down. The mainline East Coast trains still stop here, although the fine, welcoming station buildings have gone. There are nesting terns in the dunes, sailing boats in the estuary and eider ducks drifting in and out on the tides, as well as pantile roofs, colour-washed terraces, solid Victorian and Edwardian houses, a dormy house for the golf course in the form of Foxton Hall and a modest club house for the ancient village links course. Whether it be the oldest, second oldest or third oldest course in the country, its situation is still sublime above a length of the empty, golden beach which stretches for two miles between Marden rocks and Birling Carrs.

Right: Alnmouth from the cross on Church Hill across the Aln estuary

live!
live!
exhibition
film
access all areas

Bexhill-on-Sea, Sussex

There is a well-behaved air about Bexhill which is surprising since, at the turn of the century, it was the first resort in Britain to promote mixed bathing. This caused shock waves at the time but it helped to advertise the brand-new resort – to the delight of its original developer, the 8th Earl De La Warr. He had already built a fashionable hotel, a series of voluptuously ornate Edwardian terraces with swooping gables, a grand Kursaal (pavilion) for indoor entertainments and a bicycling boulevard along the seafront for fitness fanatics. De La Warr was a natural showman and publicist. In 1902 he staged the very first motor races ever held in Britain. A crowd of four thousand gathered to watch the race from Galley Hill to the Kursaal, among them H S Rolls, Louis Renault and Herbert Austin.

The Kursaal is long gone and has been replaced by Bexhill Sailing Club, its members' boats pulled up beyond the high tide-line onto the shingle. Further along, past cherry-red cast-iron shelters and white beach huts ('We'd never have coloured ones, far too garish,' a local told me), there are some onion-domed cottages whose long back gardens stretch to the beach, each fiercely competing with the next, their styles ranging from minimal box balls to red-hot pokers in crazy paving. The colonnade next door curves in an elegant semicircle back from the sea and is topped by two round temples above the promenade. Directly behind them is Bexhill's *pièce de résistance*, the De La Warr Pavilion. If the 8th Earl De La Warr liked to keep his Bexhill visitor exclusive, then the 9th had different ideas altogether. A staunch socialist, he and the corporation set about replacing the lost Kursaal with a 'People's Palace'. Out of two hundred entrants, Serge Chermayeff and Erich Mendelsohn won the architectural competition to design the first welded steel-frame building in the country, a bold example of the International Modernist style. Many residents were appalled by the pavilion's appearance when it was built in 1935, but today it shines bright. Despite the 9th Earl's socialist expectations for the pavilion, its recent renaissance has engendered an expensive restaurant, and in the great auditorium it shows art movies and performances which verge on the highbrow. In the end Bexhill-on-Sea has hung onto its exclusivity: it has even held slot machines at bay.

Main: the De La Warr Pavilion
Inset: a red cast-iron shelter in front of De La Warr Parade

Blackpool, Lancashire

Blackpool is gaudy and straightforward and affords as much entertainment as you can pack into a town. It is not for the faint-hearted: though she rather enjoyed it when she stayed here in 1980, Mrs A J P Taylor pronounced: 'In Blackpool everything serves low tastes.' Blackpool is Lancashire's answer to Brighton: there is a constant party atmosphere.

Early seaside enthusiasts first came to what was called 'Mr Forshaw's bathing place' in 1730: the easy slope of the safe, sandy beach was just what the doctor ordered. Structural progress was slow through the nineteenth century, but when holidaying Lancastrians from Manchester and Liverpool, Bolton, Preston and Oldham could reach Blackpool by train, its success was guaranteed and its popularity has never faded.

Everything about Blackpool's Victorian and Edwardian pleasure buildings was bold, brave and often pioneering. Its very first light display was in 1879 and the more elaborate festooning of the Promenade became part of Blackpool's brilliance in 1912 to coincide with a royal visit. The sturdy, attention-grabbing tower, designed by Mr Eiffel, sits on top of what looks like a slightly squashed version of Harrods, which contains easily the most beautiful ballroom in the country.

Blackpool hung on to its Winter Gardens when all about were losing theirs, and today it houses two theatres, the Baronial, Renaissance and Spanish halls and the Empress Ballroom. Along the promenade where the famous tramline runs – one of the oldest electric tramways in the world – there are three piers jammed full of elaborate entertainments, including a Ferris wheel. At the southern end the Pleasure Beach Fairground has the most terrifying roller coaster imaginable. The locals refer to it simply as 'The Big One'.

Most of the buildings along the front are modest and were not built for swank, but there are sudden bursts of fantasy, like Coral Island, an amusement arcade topped with a giant pirate's skull, and the flamboyant Metropole Hotel. There is a fine obelisk cenotaph, a huge glitter ball, a modern whale sculpture and the enormous Edwardian Convalescent Home for Miners set back from the greensward and now converted into flats.

Main: Blackpool Tower and illuminations at night. Inset: the Tower Ballroom, scene of some of the BBC's *Strictly Come Dancing* shows

PEPSI
AMUSEMENTS

SHERLEE

Bridlington, Yorkshire

'Are you going to Brid or Scar?' asked my neighbour on the train as it drew out of York Station. 'Brid,' I replied. 'Grand,' she said. Bridlington is cosy, comfortable and on a smaller scale than Scarborough. On its southern edges there is a 1950s air: privet hedges guard chunky, stalwart red-roofed villas on Kingston Road as it curls round to join Marine Drive down on the front. David Hockney chose to live at this end of town, where all is solid, friendly and down-to-earth. The words carved on the pavement read, 'Since 1806 the light from Flamborough Head has swept its great arc over dark and dangerous seas.' Today the distant lighthouse on its mighty promontory of chalk-white cliffs gives four flashes of light every sixteen seconds. In the lee of the headland, Bridlington harbour, with its plain little pier, noses out into the bay and divides the town's two beaches – North Sands, which ends in the white boulders below Sewerby's cliffs, and the wonderful deep sweep of South Sands, which stretches for miles to empty dunes and the lost, ancient village of Auburn, which was washed away by the sea.

Bridlington is realistic about its bad weather. In the shadow of a beautifully preserved and faded Victorian crescent there are glassed-in pubs and cafés hanging over the sea, while Leisure World nearby provides what the brochure calls 'a piece of the Mediterranean in Bridlington'. The Spa, an ambitious entertainment complex which opened in 1896 to the strains of Herr Meyer Lutz's Grand Band, has had yet another face-lift. Its faintly Moorish front is now shiny bright, its theatre 'updated' and its glittering, galleried ballroom in 1930s guise awaits the stars. (I heard Eric Clapton playing here in 1976.) A traditional holiday resort of the mining community, Bridlington has always been well loved by Yorkshire people, but the jolly seaside culture for which it is famous is being mildly eroded by over-zealous regenerators. On the front the familiar civic flower beds in Pembroke Gardens have been replaced by a hard landscape set with what looks like a series of plate-glass windows. From the new concrete benches you can no longer watch the waves over the sea wall.

A world apart, the sinuous streets of the old town lie well back from the quay and radiate from the remains of one of the greatest Augustinian priories in Yorkshire. St John of Bridlington (the last English saint to be canonised before the Reformation) performed his miracles here, including the saving of the lives of five Hartlepool sailors. When they prayed to God as their ship was about to be wrecked around Flamborough Head, John appeared to them and steered them safely into the harbour.

Left: Bridlington quayside

Brighton, Sussex

Brighton has always been exciting. In 1782 Fanny Burney described plunging into the sea here at 6 am on a November morning 'by the pale blink of the moon', and two years later when 'Prinny' (who later became the Prince Regent) first came to stay here with his fast-living uncle, the Duke of Cumberland (who ran a gaming house and started Brighton Races), he was smitten. The world and his wife followed him. Away from the formal strictures of court life in London, it was the feeling of freedom Prinny loved, in what was then a small town of old inns, winding streets and twittens around the Steine, an area of low ground with a stream (now a rarefied shopping area, the Lanes). The home he built, the Brighton Pavilion, enlarged and enhanced over the next forty years in the form of an exotic mogul fairytale palace, reflected his passion for pleasurable indulgences as well as his defiance of convention. Brighton was never judgmental. It still isn't. It remains the most tolerant town in the land and one in which it is impossible to be a misfit.

The hottest Regency and Victorian property-developers and entrepreneurs cashed in on the fashionable craze for Brighton and set about building a kind of Belgravia-on-Sea, seamlessly expanding into Hove. Stately buttercream or white stucco set pieces sprang up – Brunswick Terrace, Regency Square, Adelaide Crescent – as well as huge, swaggering hotels like the Grand and the Metropole along the front. Glorious churches ended street views – St George's, All Saints, St Bartholomew's and St Michael's and All Angels – while the designs for the station and piers were the best that money could buy.

Brighton's sensational downland setting was its making. Its gradual spread was easily absorbed over the undulating hills, from large council estates to lavish mock-Tudor homes. Its growth has not detracted from its beauty. It is still a thrill to look down the steep slope of Montpelier Place, past the pretty balconies, and see the sea's horizon halfway up the sky.

Brighton's past is its present. The spirit of freedom, which began with Prinny, continues. Despite the enormous influx of middle-class families who have settled here, Brighton is still as edgy as it ever was – 'the twisted piece of wire' of Graham Greene's *Brighton Rock*.

Main: sunbathers on deckchairs near the Palace Pier
Inset: Brighton Pavilion

ELECTRICIANS ?

Broadstairs, Kent

On May 29th 1974 the *Broadstairs and St Peter's Mail* reported on its front page that the charms of Broadstairs had at last reached the stars: 'The actor Gregory Peck has promised to visit the town next time he is in England.' But Peck never kept his promise and today Broadstairs remains in comfortable obscurity, sandwiched between its large, rumbustious neighbours, Ramsgate and Margate. Its beaches are wonderful – Botany Bay and Joss Bay have golden sands and chalk-white cliffs peppered with smugglers' tunnel entrances, while the beach directly below the heart of town is sheltered and intimate.

The Isle of Thanet juts out like a fist into the sea and, until the railways came, was a place apart – its glories accessible only to richer holidaymakers who could afford the travel costs. The advent of trains brought thousands of day-tripping Londoners, but of the three resorts Broadstairs was always the quietest and the most select.

It was misty and drizzling as I walked from the station down towards the front, but I felt at home. Beside the Albion Hotel an alley leads through to the first thrilling sight of the sea and, set high above it, the Parade, a satisfying curve of Georgian and Regency houses of disparate styles, with balconies and little iron-railed gardens stretching to the pavement and the balustrade above the beach. The absence of cars is luxurious. Apart from the sound of the sea, there is silence.

The first house on the Parade belonged to Mary Pearson Strong, upon whom Dickens based his character Betsey Trotwood. Dickens loved Broadstairs and stayed here every summer from 1837 until the late 1850s. He wrote *David Copperfield* in Fort House, a grand castellated villa high above the harbour. (Wilkie Collins subsequently rented it and found inspiration for *The Woman in White* from the handsome white lighthouse on North Foreland point.) 'We must reluctantly admit,' Dickens wrote in 'Our English Watering-Place', when he realised how the railways had brought a different class of visitor to Broadstairs, 'that the time when this pretty little semicircular sweep of houses ... was a gay place, and when the lighthouse overlooking it shone at daybreak on company dispersing from public balls, is but dimly traditional now.'

At its northern end the Parade slopes down towards Harbour Street. Part of the original fishing community, it wanders below Fort House and flaunts a grand little knapped flint, pedimented cinema. Under a sixteenth-century flint arch, the way leads to what Dickens described as the 'queer old wooden pier, fortunately without the slightest pretensions to architecture and very picturesque in consequence.'

Right: Fort House (now called Bleak House) which overlooks Viking Bay at Broadstairs

THE PAVILION
GARDEN ON THE SANDS

Bude, Cornwall

Bude is low-key, low-lying and sporty. The links golf course (founded in 1891), which undulates across the humpy grass-topped dunes, is bounded by the town and the sea. It feels as though it was designed as a public park, and gives Bude an open, airy feel. Most famously, Bude boasts the best surf for miles around. The beach is the thing – three miles of booming Atlantic rollers thunder in along the shining low-tide sands. If you stand mid-way you can hear the ever-constant sound of the distant surf, coupled with a different note played by the River Strat as it rushes over flat pebbles and widens out onto Summerleaze Beach. Walking back towards the shore, a sheltering arm of lowish, biscuit-coloured cliff curls around you: together with a strong sea wall it forms Bude Haven.

The small fishing village mushroomed when it became the seaport of the Bude Canal and little cottages sprang up among the old along Breakwater Road, well hunkered down against the gales. The canal's final lock gates end in the tidal harbour beside the widening Strat, and today the two waterways still run parallel through the flat valley to Helebridge. The canal was an ambitious project conceived by the Cornishman John Edyvean in 1774 to carry sand inland for fertilising fields, as well as distributing coal from Wales. It was finally built thirty years later at a cost of £120,000, and at various points along its twenty-mile course to Launceston, the barges (which were fitted with wheels) were pulled up the inclines by steam engines. When the railway finally reached Bude at the end of the century, the canal's trade began to fall away and by the 1960s much of the waterway had disappeared under the plough and excavator.

The resort side of Bude was helped along by the presence of Sir Thomas Acland, who lived in the ancient manor of Ebbingford, and his friend Sir Goldsworthy Gurney, a gentleman inventor who built an elaborate sham castle overlooking Summerleaze Beach in the 1830s. Apart from inventing possibly the first-ever steam road locomotive, he also created an early form of illumination, 'the Bude Light', by forcing oxygen into a naked flame. He caused quite a stir among the early holidaymakers, but Bude was still remote and the town's development was modest. Today there are handsome stucco terraces beside the golf course on the Flexbury side of town and Edwardian hotels on the bluff above Summerleaze, and from the sun deck of the Life's A Beach café you can watch the brave high-tide surfers taking off from the rocks into Bude's famously good, clean swell.

Main: Summerleaze Beach
Inset: a local chip-shop sign

Budleigh Salterton, Devon

Spindly pine trees top little rounded hills as the River Otter widens to the sea. It ends in a small, heron-haunted archipelago of reedy marsh behind the bank of beach at Budleigh Salterton. From here you can see the two-and-a-half-mile-long bay stretching in an imperceptible arc to the west beyond the bright red sandstone cliffs to distant Otter Cove.

There is a clarity and neatness about Budleigh beach. But everything about Budleigh is neat – even its perfectly smooth, soft-to-the-touch pebbles, which can be traced back 440 million years. In shades of mauvish and pinkish grey, some of them are as big as goose eggs. They are composed of a hard quartzite brought here from Brittany by one of the giant rivers flowing into the Triassic desert. For the last few thousand years the pebbles have been falling off the cliffs onto the beach and have been a perfect quarry for ornament around the town. You see them everywhere in cottage and garden walls.

Budleigh feels homely and well-heeled. With its barn-like red-tiled roof, the late Victorian church, the gift of a local grandee, could be in Surrey. Cole's the Butcher, Richard's Menswear and Gulliver's Books on the High Street are typical of the town's independent shops, and their owners are proud to have kept the ubiquitous chains at bay. The town is comfortably tucked into the lower slopes of Shortwood Common and West Down, its inter-war villas and bungalows settled around the outskirts. At its heart are grand little Regency houses, a pretty late-Georgian bow-windowed terrace off Fore Street Hill, and here and there a scattering of *cottages ornés*, vestiges of Budleigh's small-time beginnings as a resort (it never took off like its neighbours, Sidmouth and Exmouth). The gothic-windowed cottage of Fairlynch (now the museum) has a double-winged staircase and a fancy thatched look-out tower perched on its roof ridge – the whim of its ship-owning builder. In 1870 the painter John Everett Millais came to stay in the Octagon, a tall conical-roofed *cottage orné*, while he painted *The Boyhood of Raleigh,* the setting of which is the seafront at Budleigh. (Raleigh was born in Hayes Barton farmhouse nearby and went to church in East Budleigh.) Many of Budleigh's twentieth-century houses are strongly influenced by the Arts and Crafts Movement, which suits the cosiness of the town. There is a particularly good row of asymmetrical, half-timbered mock-medieval houses beside 'The Lawn'.

Main: Budleigh beach. Inset: Fairlynch cottage

Clevedon, **Somerset**

Clevedon is classy. It stands aloof from its workmanlike neighbour, Portishead, and huddles against wooded hills, cut off from the world on a thin slither of land between the moaning motorway and the Severn estuary. Across the estuary, muddy and buff-coloured from a storm, Newport is just visible against the rise of Welsh hills on the opposite bank.

When you first arrive in Clevedon from wooded gorges and the shadow of hills, you have no sense of the sea, and it's a shock to suddenly find yourself out on the blustery front, where the little bandstand looks as though it will take off and the Scots pines in the public gardens are bent horizontal by the wind. To stand on the bluff above Little Harp Bay, with a low wall between you and the water below, is exactly like being on the deck of a liner: when the tide is high it races by at such a speed that you feel you are moving along.

When Alfred Tennyson's best-loved friend Arthur Hallam died of a brain haemorrhage at the age of twenty-two in Vienna, he was brought to Clevedon to be buried – which Tennyson described so movingly in 'In Memoriam'. Arthur was a relation of the Eltons of Clevedon Court, the art-loving family who were behind much of the reserved and enlightened planning of the resort side of Clevedon. Lamb, Landor, Tennyson and Thackeray were constant visitors to their ancient house, half hidden under the wooded Warren behind the town. Sir Arthur Elton was a leading light in the building of Clevedon Pier in 1869. A hundred years later, when its future was in jeopardy, the Clevedon Pier Society was formed and my father was quoted as deeming it 'the most beautiful pier in the country'. A massive £100,000 was raised towards its restoration. Today it is back to its full glory and is listed Grade 1.

The seafront boasts handsome houses with Regency names like Adelaide, Brunswick and Clarence, and up the wooded slopes the slate-roofed, grey-stone Victorian villas command ever better views. But if you climb higher to the seventeenth-century octagonal hunting lodge and the golf course on Castle Hill, three hundred feet up, you get the best view of all. You can see the drifts of woodland all over the hills undulating back to Clifton, and the voluptuously wooded indents of the estuary beyond Wains Hill at the southern end of Clevedon.

Right: Clevedon Pier

Criccieth, Caernarfonshire

It was early evening when I drove to Criccieth. On the far side of Porthmadog Bay, Harlech Castle was just discernible below the high blue horizons of Snowdonia, rising in undulating outlines. There are few landscapes more beautiful. Travelling down Lon Fel to the shore, the first sight of Criccieth Castle, romantic and melancholy, perched high on its sea-girt rocky promontory, stopped me in my tracks. 'The two fortresses [Criccieth and Harlech] seem to be in constant watch over one another,' Lindsay Evans writes in *The Castles of Wales*, 'weather permitting, for in this part of Wales, the moody light plays the most theatrical tricks on both land and seascapes.'

Here the gallant Sir Hywel of the Axe, appointed constable of the castle by the Black Prince in 1359, gained a legendary reputation for bravery and was hymned by the court poet:

Shaving with mighty blow on blow
The head and beard of many a foe,
And shedding lightly, yea, foot high
The blood of any his strength would try.

The castle was half ruined a century later but the town, which had grown in its shadow with pebbled pavements and little houses made from huge blocks of the local stone, continued to mushroom towards the hills and around the two beautiful beaches. To the west of the castle promontory Marine Terrace, chock-a-block with bay-windowed bed-and-breakfasts painted in different ice-cream shades, faces the lovely, wide, shingly, bladderwrack-strewn beach, which sweeps on round towards Pwllheli. Down the steep hill on the eastern side of the castle, past the jaunty lifeboat building with its bright scarlet half timbering and bargeboards, the Esplanade curves around East Beach with small Edwardian hotels and council houses on a terrace above it. Beyond, the small emerald hills are scattered with sheep, rocky outcrops and clumps of gorse. At the far end of the beach, where the sand merges with rocks and pools, there is a café looking like a mini lido in jazz modern style, designed by local architect Clough Williams-Ellis in 1954 (as different to his Portmeirion up the road as you could get).

Criccieth is a quiet, modest place boasting only of its famous son, Lloyd George, who worked here for a firm of solicitors in his youth. (He was brought up in a cottage nearby.) The bulk of the little market town is centred around a wide, sloping green which, twice a year, is the scene of the ancient Criccieth Fair.

Right: Criccieth Castle above East Beach

TEAS
BLUE CHINA

Cromer, Norfolk

Cromer is a magical place. Approaching it from the heights of Roughton Heath, you suddenly see the town way below against a backdrop of slate-blue sea – all red pantile roofs, cedar trees, pinnacled Victorian and Edwardian houses, flamboyant verandahs on the edges of the old town, and then the great flint church of St Peter and St Paul, flaunting Norfolk's highest tower at its heart.

Crab stalls are everywhere, and steep steps and zig-zagging pebble-walled ramps lead down to East and West Beach, which curve away in a long slow arc of golden sand from either side of the pier. Despite its spectacular position, Cromer is no longer the playground of the phenomenally rich that it once was. Gone are the days when the cream of London society dipped down for summer sojourns, when Elizabeth of Austria took a wing of Tucker's Hotel, when the Maharajah of Cooch Behar resided on Clifford Avenue, when Edward VII is whispered to have stayed with Lillie Langtry in the Hôtel de Paris, when local landowner Lord Suffield made a golf course for the top brass, and Norfolk's richest families – the Barclays, Hoares, Hastings, Buxtons and Gurneys – built holiday houses here. 'The certain fashion at this pretty little waterside place is religiously obeyed,' a visitor to Cromer wrote in 1886. 'It is the rule to go on the sands in the morning, to walk on one cliff for a mile in the afternoon, to take another mile in the other direction and at sunset to crowd upon the little pier at night.'

Pierre le François, the son of a French baron who had fled to England to escape the Revolution, saw that Cromer was lacking in classy establishments, bought a private villa on the seafront and ran it as a boarding house, the Hôtel de Paris. It was an instant success. When the railway came in 1877 and brought the promise of more visitors, the highly inventive Norwich architect, George Skipper, got the plum jobs – the Town Hall, the Grand Hotel and the Hotel Metropole – but his rebuild of the Hôtel de Paris is his lasting monument to Edwardian individualism. It towers ruby-red above the silvery walls of Jetty Cliff at the apex of the seafront, and commands a dead-on view of Cromer pier, the last in the land to stage a live show every night in its Pavilion Theatre. From the end of the pier you can watch the crab boats coming in as they have done since the town's first beginnings. Cromer crabs are the best in the world.

Main: the view from Cromer Pier with the Hôtel de Paris on the right. Inset: Cromer crabs on sale

Dawlish, Devon

Above Dawlish, the narrow road drops down from the sandy heath into a steep darkness of fir trees and laurels which conceals pheasant-thick country estates on either side. At the foot of the hill, where Dawlish Water runs beside the road, there is a lodge and the glimpse of a parkland drive. In 1797 the fabulously rich banker Charles Hoare chose this small valley as his favourite site in England, and employed John Nash to build an ornamental castle and Humphry Repton to landscape its park. Dawlish's reputation as a fashionable resort went up several notches.

In 1803 John Manning, an enterprising local businessman, realised that development behind Dawlish beach was limited by the massive red sandstone cliffs at either end. He decided to make Dawlish Water the focal point of the resort instead. From the top of the old village and through the chestnut-shaded green he straightened the course of the meandering brook into a shallow and formal canal with waterfalls and bridges running straight as a die to the beach. Small, informal Regency houses were built either side of the watercourse with a generous greensward in front of them. The little town grew around the surrounding amphitheatre of hills, and today the wide band of public park in the middle, with its elegant cream and green shelters and its canal dotted with black swans, is what gives Dawlish its special flavour. Jane Austen was enchanted by the place and set it as the scene of Lucy and Ferrars's honeymoon in *Sense and Sensibility*. Dickens stayed here when he was settling his mother into a new house nearby and as a result made Dawlish the birthplace of Nicholas Nickleby.

The commercial success of nearly every resort in Britain depended on the railway. In Dawlish's case, Brunel's original 'atmospheric' railway not only came, it devoured one of town's major assets, the beautiful red-sand beach, by marching across it on the lowest of viaducts. (The hundreds of navvies shipped in to build the line and to tunnel through the cliffs caused great excitement with local tradesmen and publicans, but the more refined residents decried their 'wanton drunkenness'.)

If you travel through Dawlish on a train today, it looks as though the town behind is cut off from the beach. But if you stand where Dawlish Water makes its formalised entrance to the sea, you can walk under the line. The railway is now part and parcel of Dawlish and adds to its quirkiness. (What Brunel had not foreseen was the corrosion of the ironwork by the sea, as a result of which the station and viaduct paintwork appear to be in a permanent state of neglect.)

Left: the railway along the sea wall at Dawlish

THE ROYAL HOTEL

Deal, Kent

Centuries of vilification left Deal unregarded. Pepys called it 'pitiful', while in 1823 Cobbett found it a 'most villainous place. It is full of filthy looking people. Great desolation of abomination has been going on here ... Every thing seems upon the perish.' Nelson deemed it the coldest place in England, and in Jane Austen's *Persuasion* Deal was the only place in England in which Admiral Croft's wife was ever ill. In the early 1950s, as part of a slum-clearance scheme, the local council planned to pull down most of Deal's pleasing seafront as well as the higgledy-piggledy streets behind. The Deal Preservation Society was formed, halted the demolition and, in consequence, the whole quarter became the first official Conservation Area in Kent. Today it is Deal's great showcase, livened up (until his death in 1988) by resident Charles Hawtrey, who paraded along it in extravagant attire with half an eye on every young male passer-by.

From the ordinary High Street, skinny alleys lead off to the sea where the sound of the waves dragging the shingle back down the sloping beach is pleasurably loud. Mid-front, what must be the ugliest pier in Britain strikes out for 102 feet towards the wreck-strewn Goodwin Sands where at low tide you can see, four miles out, waves breaking across the treacherous bar. Way down at the end of the pier, where the nice Norwegian-style café looks like the skeleton of a boat, you can gaze back at Deal and see that its straight, unadulterated front is not only magnificent, but also unlike anything else in England. Its eighteenth- and early nineteenth-century cottages and small houses were built for seamen or those connected with the sea, and they look onto Deal's *raison d'être*, the 'Downs', the long stretch of deep, sheltered waters where up to eight hundred vessels at a time could anchor during stormy or calm weather.

Deal is one of the ancient order of Cinque Ports. Its perfect little castle on the western end of town lies low and neat, set beyond the wedding cake-like Prince of Wales Terrace, one of Deal's few contributions to resort architecture. Beyond, where the wide stretch of shingle is dotted with mallow between beached boats, the handsome nineteenth-century naval barracks, for over sixty years the home of the Royal Marines School of Music, are set back from the sea. On 22nd September 1989 the IRA blew up part of it and the bandstand on the greensward ahead (where the edges of Deal and Walmer blur) was built to the memory of the eleven bandsmen who were killed.

Main: Deal seafront. Inset: the bandstand

WINGS
APPEAL

Eastbourne, Sussex

A native of Eastbourne told me that on returning from time away, the first view of the town from the downs of Beachy Head never failed to bring a lump to her throat. As a non-native I had the same feeling. I was amazed at seeing the place for the first time in its gigantic wooded bowl with the shining sea ahead. Although the town now sprawls inland for almost five miles, and an ill-fitting 1960s tower block commands the bay, looking hopelessly out of place, Eastbourne is still a cause for wonder. Harold Pinter may have described it as seamy in *The Birthday Party* (having stayed here as a jobbing actor in the early 1950s), but many more have loved it, including Tommy Cooper, Charlie Chester and Debussy, who wrote most of *La Mer* while staying in the Grand Hotel.

I went when the sun shone, the band played, and I felt uplifted. It is the boldness and the opulent scale of the original concept which hits you. Before JCBs had been thought of, a mile and a half of virgin land sloping to the shoreline was cut into and levelled off to create an extravagantly generous three-tiered promenade between the grandest of sparkling white terraces and the sea. The seventh Duke of Devonshire, who was the major landowner, charged the architect Henry Currey to plan 'a town by gentlemen, for gentlemen', with tree-lined boulevards, squares, terraces, hotels and villas. Stringent planning restrictions were left in place in order to safeguard the integrity of the original plan. All the seafront buildings are white – no colours are allowed.

Back from the sea, Eastbourne College (opened in 1867), the minimalist Towner Gallery and an elegant eighteenth-century house, Compton Place, in its leafy park, lend distinction to the town – but it is the brilliant set piece of Eastbourne's front which is its glory. The civic colour scheme of blue and white looks beautiful on all the seaside railings, and still further enhances Eugenius Birch's sensational pier. Exotic floral sculptures, carpet bedding and feathery pampas grass plantings proliferate along the promenade. You can sit in the shade of a colonnade beside the turquoise-roofed bandstand, as recommended by the late Duke of Devonshire, who wrote: 'The combination of military music and crashing breakers is far more intoxicating than any alcohol.'

Main: the front at Eastbourne
Inset: Fusciardi's ice cream parlour

Falmouth, Cornwall

'The simple truth is that in Falmouth it is as warm in January as it is in Madrid, and as cool in July as it is in Petrograd. There is an incontrovertible fact for you.' So reads an extract from the *Cornish Riviera* published in 1928 by the Great Western Railway Company. Falmouth is at the estuary of seven rivers, frayed with inlets and creeks, and guarded by two forts built by Henry VIII: St Mawes Castle across the mouth of the Fal, and the mighty Pendennis Castle on the Falmouth side. The castle sits high on a long verdant promontory, with steep wooded slopes falling away below the long stretches of gun emplacements.

Although it has grown into one of Cornwall's largest towns, Falmouth still has all the stirring romance of a Patrick O'Brian novel. In the old heart of it there are sudden glimpses of water and the noise of clinking masts. For two hundred years, it was the last stopping place for ships sailing west across the Atlantic and the first port of call for those homeward-bound. Its sheltered harbour is the third deepest in the world. Falmouth Packets, built locally and owned by the Post Office, carried all our overseas mail as far as the West Indies, and the town was the first place in Britain to learn of Nelson's victory at Trafalgar. Georgian houses, Regency terraces and the handsome Doric customs house tell of those times. When the Post Office decided to use steam ships instead, they transferred their business to Liverpool and Southampton and the town's prosperity and importance as a harbour declined.

The railway came in 1863 and a group of local speculators earmarked the best site of all above the unspoilt Castle Beach and overlooking Pendennis Point. Two years later they built the Falmouth Hotel in a sumptuous French château style and Castle Drive was laid out – perhaps the most beautiful coastal drive in England. Visitors were attracted by Falmouth's cliffs, wooded slopes and headlands, sub-tropical ravine gardens touched by the Gulf Stream, rock pools and, above all, its warmth. Helped along by the Fox family of Quakers and well strewn with luxuriant public gardens, resort development mushroomed along Cliff Road and around Falmouth's wealth of fine beaches – Tunnel, Gyllyngvase, Swanpool and Maenporth.

Florence Nightingale came to stay at the Greenbanks Hotel, as did Kenneth Grahame. It was from here that he began writing *The Wind in the Willows* to his son, in letter form, in 1907. Poldark's creator, Winston Graham, lived in the White Cottage on Fenwick Street and set his novel *The Forgotten Story* in Falmouth.

Right: the Falmouth Hotel above Castle Beach

FALMOUTH HOTEL

Filey, Yorkshire

Beyond the ghost of a 1939 Butlin's Holiday Camp, where only the huge, empty swimming pool and its tiered fountain survive among the scrubland, Filey retains an air of quiet, solid respectability. Past a roundabout packed with scarlet roses, pale apricot brick terraces and white stucco bay-windowed pubs and inns, only the sea is visible – the beach is hidden far below the cliff-like hill. There was a high spring tide running down on the front when I went, and the sand was completely covered. 'The sea is very grand,' Charlotte Brontë wrote to her father from a lodging house in Filey in 1852. 'Yesterday was a somewhat unusually high tide, and I stood about an hour on the cliffs yesterday afternoon watching the tumbling in of great tawny, turbid waves, that made the whole shore white with foam and filled the air with a sound hollower and deeper than thunder.'

The retaining wall which fortifies the Beach Road is built with enormous blocks of grim grey stone, bulging into a curved secure bastion above the Coble – a slipway for the crab, lobster and 'Filey salmon' fishing boats.

Yorkshire's middle classes have long chosen to holiday here rather than in more colourful Scarborough. There isn't the breath of an amusement arcade on the front. 'The Swedish Nightingale' Jenny Lind, the composer Frederick Delius, the pianist Myra Hess and the Mountbatten family all spent summers here, perhaps in the proud stucco terraces facing out to sea from the top of the cliff or down the steep loop of cobbled road in the handsome row of biscuit-coloured stone houses and stucco hotels set back behind the greensward on Beach Road.

Back from the Brigg, a natural rock promontory, rise the great boulder clay cliffs of Carr Naze. On low spring tides an ancient black rock breakwater, known as the Spittals, is revealed – thought by some locals to be Roman. (In consequence a cave at the back of the Brigg is called the 'Emperor's Bath'.) Fathoms below, there are wrecks lurking off the point, including – it is thought – that of the American *Bonhomme Richard*, which sank here in a sea battle in 1779 under the captaincy of John Paul Jones.

Main: Filey from the cliffs on the north side
Inset: the sign for the Coble Landing Bar by the beach

Fowey, Cornwall

Fowey is all romance. The town's face and its heroic history as one of Cornwall's principal ports was, and is, its fortune. There are steep twisting streets of whitewashed cottages, their pattern unchanged since medieval times; a triple-aisled church at its heart, stuffed with monuments to the Rashleighs of Menabilly and the Treffrys, whose ancient pile 'Place', with its battlemented walls and turrets, overshadows the churchyard. There are old inns like The Ship and the flashily handsome King of Prussia, which takes centre stage on Albert Quay, with its glistening granite steps and its Doric columns; and there are the magical wooded creeks winding to secret places along the estuary.

Fowey's quaintness remains intact despite the Victorian speculators' terraces, the grand Fowey Hotel and a veritable palace called Fowey Hall, which crowd the steep hillside towards the open sea. Arthur Quiller-Couch (1863–1944) 'discovered' Fowey and in 1892 moved to the Haven, just beyond the little sandy sweep of Readymoney Cove. He did much to enhance the desirability of the town through his novels, which were often set in Fowey, and gradually it became the haunt of artistic people. In 1927 the actor-manager Gerald du Maurier bought a holiday hideaway called Ferryside in the tiny hamlet of Bodinnick which looks across to Fowey from the eastern side of the river. It was here that his daughter Daphne wrote many of her novels, which are redolent of Fowey, its families and its surroundings. 'When I first arrived at Ferryside,' she wrote, 'I would seize every opportunity to explore, to walk for miles – bluebells everywhere – or cross the ferry to Fowey, walk through the town, and so to the castle on the cliff above the harbour mouth. Soon I discovered with fascination the enchanted woods on Gribben headland ...' It was there that she found her 'house of secrets' in the hidden and deserted Menabilly, and eventually rented it from the Rashleigh family for thirty years. It became the setting for *Rebecca*: 'Last night I dreamt I went to Manderley again ... Time could not wreck the perfect symmetry of those walls, nor the site itself, a jewel in the hollow of a hand.'

Even without the presence of Fowey's famous children, the headland landscape, the penny royal in the alley walls around the churchyard, the grassy tea garden terrace below the Fowey Hotel, which looks towards the grey roofs of the little town of Polruan across the water, and the lichen-encrusted woods around Readymoney Cove would captivate any romantic heart.

Main: Fowey in the evening light
Inset: Readymoney Cove

Frinton-on-Sea, Essex

Frinton has a reputation for being quiet (a recent advert included the lines: 'Am I dead?' 'No, you're in Frinton-on-Sea'). The residents' association is a powerful force. There are no shops along the front and only one hotel. The golf club, founded in 1885, commands the western end of Frinton and successfully blocks any development towards Clacton. The thatched half-timbered tennis club next door, founded a few years later, has an air of exclusivity. Its fabled tennis fortnight in June on the perfect grass courts at the bottom of Holland Road used to be second only to Wimbledon. It is still attended by the likes of Cliff Richard and Sue Barker, I was told. At the junction of Holland Road and Second Avenue, the Homestead – one of architect Charles Voysey's best houses – seems to grow organically from its sloping corner site: the very epitome of romantic homeliness. It is only one of the sumptuous villas at this, the poshest end of Frinton. Every one is a gem, particularly Marylands, where Edward VIII and Mrs Simpson often stayed, along with Douglas Fairbanks and Gladys Cooper. Frinton is discreet. My local guide told me confidentially that Roger Moore's father used to live there, and he also showed me the black clapboarded cricket club, hidden away from the world off First Avenue up an unmarked track. It stands amidst beautiful and unadulterated rural Essex with Great Holland church tower rising from the near horizon.

The Grand Hotel (now apartments), along with the golf club, saw the beginning of Frinton's development as a resort. The buildings are set well back from the sea and the Greensward, a wide stretch of common land high above the beach which sweeps along Frinton's seafront from one end to the other and lends it calm. Connaught Avenue followed on, the main artery from the railway station to the Esplanade. Affectionately known as the 'Bond Street of East Anglia', it is lined with restrained Edwardian red-brick shops, some in the Queen Anne style of the time.

In complete contrast to the Edwardian splendour of Frinton's posh southern end, a daring modernist scheme was planned for the northern end in 1934. The architect Oliver Hill was commissioned to design the Frinton Park Estate, which was to be a showcase of the very latest jazz modern style. The public were not ready for it, and only a dozen or so houses were built of the thousand planned. Today they stand out as shining stars along the esplanade or among the avenues of bungalows on the fuzzy edges of neighbouring Walton on the Naze. The latter, with the second longest pier in Britain, is looked down on by Frinton folk.

Main: one of Oliver Hill's houses
Inset: the beach at Frinton-on-Sea

Grange-over-Sands, Cumbria

Grange is on the mysterious Cartmel Peninsula, its low-lying edges often wreathed in mist. I came on a train from Carnforth beside the vast expanse of Morecambe Bay, and crossed the treacherous sands of the Kent estuary on a stalwart Victorian viaduct of fifty spans. Grange Station is beautiful. Its elaborate wrought ironwork, supporting the glass platform canopies, is painted red and apple-green – colours echoed in the gardens of nearby villas. Grange is a luxuriantly verdant place set among the foothills of Hampsfell and Yewbarrow Woods, and faces out over salt marshes and the high-tide water to Silverdale. The town's sheltered position makes it warmer in spring than anywhere else in the north of England. Semi-tropical plants and shrubs thrive in the Ornamental Gardens around a lake; and for over a mile the gently snaking promenade is edged with constantly changing planting schemes, from alpine rockeries to voluptuous herbaceous borders, all tended by volunteers from the town.

Grange used to be virtually inaccessible – the roads were famously bad, and in the early 1800s only a handful of adventurous visitors came, attracted by the mild climate and the new cult of sea bathing. They stayed in the inn or rented cottages from locals. The coming of the railways in 1857 changed everything and saw this once remote hamlet transformed into a discreet and rarefied Victorian resort – with gabled and barge-boarded houses and hotels, all built of the local limestone. A raised promenade was constructed along the sea's edge, but in the last century the sea changed its course and today only covers the mosses and sheep-grazed salt marshes at spring tides.

The way the tides twist and turn in the shifting sands makes even the shortest crossings highly dangerous; there is quicksand which can suck you down. The graves at nearby Cartmel Priory tell of countless lives lost and the tragic drowning of twenty-three Chinese cockle pickers in 2004 will not be quickly forgotten. Since the 1500s there has been an official Queen's Guide to the Sands to escort travellers. Cedric Robinson, who as a boy fished the bay with a horse and cart, dragging a net to catch cockles, shrimps, mussels and flukes, is the current title holder and lives in Grange. Carrying a stout stick to test the depths, he takes parties of intrepid walkers across the bay, and once guided Prince Philip in his carriage and four from Kents Bank to Arnside.

Main: the Ornamental Gardens
Inset: Park Road Gardens bandstand

Hunstanton, Norfolk

There are ink-black splashes of woodland on the edges of huge cereal fields in this wide-skied stretch of Norfolk where Old Hunstanton lies back from the sea. A small lane trickles down beside the church to the kempt Arts and Crafts clubhouse overlooking the golf links. The village retains the olde worlde character which Henry Le Strange, the Squire of Hunstanton Hall and Lord High Admiral of the Wash, so loved. When Le Strange, an architect manqué and the painter of Ely Cathedral's nave ceiling, planned a new resort in the 1840s, he wanted it set apart from his village.

New Hunstanton was built a mile away, high above the best bit of Norfolk coast. Huge seaweed-covered boulders are scattered across firm sand, and secret rock pools lie below the amazing cliffs which look like Battenberg cake, layered in white and red chalk and marmalade-coloured carr stone. L P Hartley loved the beach as a child and used it as his background for *The Shrimp and the Anemone*.

The heart of New Hunstanton was laid out back from the sea around a triangular green where, in 1846, Le Strange placed an old village cross to start things off and lend a sense of place to the new resort. His great friend William Butterfield, who helped him with the overall scheme, was probably responsible for its first building, the Royal Hotel (now the Golden Lion), built in the local carr stone. Other key buildings followed, including a smart town hall and a workman-like church built of flint rubble striped through with bold bands of orange stone. In the church's south-east corner there is a stained glass window by Ninian Comper depicting the fourteen-year-old St Edmund landing at Hunstanton.

There is an open and uncluttered feeling to Hunstanton, with its handsome tree-filled squares of Edwardian houses facing the edge of the Wash, and its wide greensward above the cliff. At this northern end of town there is a strong feel of Norfolk, but as the cliffs begin to taper down to the low-lying southern end, that disappears. The pier has gone and has been replaced by a swoopy entertainment centre which looks like an awkwardly beached whale.

Main: Hunstanton's red and white cliffs
Inset: the town sign in front of the Golden Lion

Ilfracombe, Devon

Ilfracombe's harbour is wrapped all around by rugged bracken-topped cliffs – the safest haven of all on the North Devon coast. It wasn't surprising that by the end of the eighteenth century a small fishing town had grown up beside the quay and back towards the ancient, low-lying church, safely settled into the hillside. Triple-aisled Holy Trinity, with its wonderful wagon roofs, reflected the increasing prosperity of the town, while St Nicholas's Chapel, which stands on a high, grey, lichen-sprinkled rock by the harbour, acted as a beacon to seafarers on one side and guarded the harbour on the other.

The town's chocolate-box setting of wooded combes winding down to secret coves, and of undulating, switchback lanes set deep between banks of hart's-tongue ferns and a hundred different wild flowers, rendered it irresistible to band-wagoning resort developers. Stylish houses sprang up in Northfield Road which connected the High Street of the old town to the new resort. There were no beaches to hand and so a team of Welsh miners was employed to tunnel through the cliff to reach suitable bathing places where separate tidal pools were provided for segregated bathing. In 1836 the tunnel entrance was adorned with a Doric temple-like building which also provided hot and cold baths. Bright new terraces – Adelaide, Hillsborough and Montpelier – clung to the precipitous hillsides. The former Clifton and Montebello hotels, tall for the time, and all tiers of balconies and bay windows, set a special Ilfracombe style.

Paddle steamers brought tourists from Wales but when the railway came in the 1870s they arrived in droves. The town spread outwards and upwards, leaving little wooded parks and greens between the houses, and gradually the whole jumble of steeply undulating hills became covered. By the end of the nineteenth century Ilfracombe was the most popular resort in North Devon.

In the 1911 edition of *Highways and Byways in Devon and Cornwall*, Arthur Norway wrote that Ilfracombe was 'a place which has grown so large of recent years that it seems to have lost all its old West Country flavour, and to have become cosmopolitan like Cowes or Brighton.' Its popularity was almost bound to fade, but Ilfracombe will always be the architectural historians' favourite – the archetypal example of seaside resort development.

The town is remembered fondly by its transient daughters, wartime evacuees Joan and Jackie Collins. It now sports the jaunty Landmark Theatre which looks like a pair of cooling towers, and has been given a new lease of life by local artist Damien Hirst, who is hoping to reawaken tourists to its splendour through his restaurant on the quay.

Right: Ilfracombe harbour

Llandudno, Caernarfonshire

High above the lush cream villas on the outskirts of Penrhyn Bay the road climbs up to the sheep-scattered heights of Little Orme's Head – all pale grey rocky outcrops and seemingly sheer grassy slopes. Over the brow, Llandudno, 'the Naples of the North', is spread out on the level land below at the narrowest point of this extraordinary peninsula. The perfect crescent shape of its northern shore is edged with an arc of graceful white stucco terraces and hotels looking out to the Irish Sea and ending in a pretty blue and white painted pier. The western shore, where Alice Liddell, the inspiration for Lewis Carroll's Alice, spent her summers as a child, looks towards Conwy Bay with its famous mussel beds. Beyond, the towering limestone headland of the Great Orme rises abruptly to nearly 700 feet. It was seized on by the Victorian developers of Llandudno as a potential honeypot for visitors. They engineered a four-mile carriage drive spiralling upwards around it, landscaped the Happy Valley gardens, built tea rooms on the Orme's summit and constructed a cable-hauled tramway to scale its heights from an elaborate, castellated station at the foot. Gabled and bargeboarded villas sprang up on the steep lower slopes of the Great Orme, their gardens stuffed with fuchsias and hydrangeas.

Main: Llandudno from the Great Orme
Inset: holidaymakers on the northern shore

From the highest path, 'Invalids' Walk', you can look down on Llandudno's grid pattern of tree-lined boulevards and the grand avenue linking the north and west beaches. The resort was planned in 1849 and the landowner Lord Mostyn's original concept is still very much intact. The main shopping area feels classy and bustling, and some of the glass canopy on its elaborate cast iron framework is still in place. According to the 1885 Murray guide Llandudno was 'much frequented by the Liverpool people'. There has been little change, although the art deco Winter Gardens, where the Beatles played to mediocre reviews in 1963, has been replaced by a block of flats.

But another art deco gem, Villa Marina, survives. Built in 1936 for £30,000, it was designed by Odeon architect Harry Weedon for Harry Scribbans, a millionaire baker from Birmingham. The baker's wife detested it, and sold it for £5,000 the moment her husband died.

Lyme Regis, **Dorset**

'An easterly is the most disagreeable wind in Lyme Bay,' writes the town's famous resident, the novelist John Fowles – 'Lyme Bay being that largest bite from the underside of England's outstretched south-western leg.' The picture he paints of the town and its immediate surroundings in *The French Lieutenant's Woman* is so vivid that even if you have never been here before, you feel you know it. As I walked along the stalwart, sinuous breakwater called the Cobb I felt I would surely see the ghost of Sarah Woodruff waiting alone at the far end.

The precariousness of the town's position is abundantly clear as one looks landward from the Cobb to the strange scalloped Undercliff scattered with trees on the western side of Lyme, and the sinister-looking cliff shelves called the Spittles to the east. Landslips are frequent – the parish church is said to be sliding towards the sea – and each one exposes the fossils of creatures which lived millions of years ago, preserved within the blue Lias clay. Mary Anning, a carpenter's daughter from Lyme, was the first to discover just how fossil-rich this stretch of the coast was. In the 1820s she found the remains of a plesiosaur, a pterosaur and a twenty-foot-long ichthyosaur. The gigantic slabs of stone which top the sloping surface of the ancient Cobb are vermiculated with tiny indentations of Jurassic burrowers and surely inspired Lyme resident Eleanor Coade, the inventor of the ceramic material known as Coade stone.

The town is beautiful, with its steep winding streets, bow windows, lampposts decorated with wrought-iron ammonites, Regency *cabane ornée* resembling a thatched igloo, gabled clapboarded houses, fossil shops, ancient inns, Nonconformist chapels, and fanciful houses along the front. A terraced public garden moulded from a landslip is thick with ferns and pampas grass. Below it, level with the beach, an amusement arcade with a grim 1970s front is set discreetly underground.

Lyme is inspiring. Whistler rented a studio here for a summer, Samuel Palmer spent time drawing the landslip and Henry Fielding dallied with a local beauty. Perhaps most famously, Jane Austen set part of *Persuasion* in Lyme. 'A very strange stranger it must be,' she remarks, 'who does not see charms in the immediate environs of Lyme to make him wish to know it better.'

Main: Town Beach, built up with imported pebbles for coastal protection. Inset: the Cobb

Lynton and Lynmouth, Devon

Lynton and Lynmouth's landscape is sublime. Vast, windswept expanses of Exmoor set with barrows, ancient earthworks and stone circles loom above, giving way to soft winding combes of hanging oak woods. Moss smothers the stone walls and the roots of beech trees, and shallow brown rivers with bouldered bottoms wind in the shade of sycamores. High above the Bristol Channel the ground falls towards the giant hog's-back cliffs. A deep, steep-wooded gorge leads down to the village of Lynmouth where, over the rocky shore, the East and West Lyn rivers meet the sea. Here, in 1952, thirty-four people died when a sudden flash flood swept down the valleys, devastating buildings and bridges in its wake.

In June 1812 the poet Shelley sped to Lynmouth with his sixteen-year-old bride Harriet Westbrook. Approaching by Countisbury Hill, he later wrote how they 'saw before and beneath them a fairy scene – Little Lynmouth, then some thirty cottages, rose-clad and myrtle-clad, nestling at the foot of the hills. It was enough.' For nine weeks they rented a cottage up from the little harbour, where Shelley finished *Queen Mab*. A radical activist, Shelley cast bottles and wax boxes containing revolutionary pamphlets out to sea and enlisted his manservant to fly-post revolutionary posters in Barnstable. The servant was arrested, and Shelley, unable to pay the fine for his release, escaped by boat to Wales, leaving scores of unpaid bills.

Lynmouth is still picturesque, with its Rhenish Tower and funicular railway up to the resort of Lynton, 500 feet above. As you travel up the precipitous slope to reach that higher world you could easily be in Switzerland. There are fir trees in the hanging woods and some of Lynton's boarding houses sport the chalet style, with deep overhanging eaves and wooden balconies. The former Royal Castle Hotel, a slate-hung Regency building with gothic glazing, commands a spectacular position above the sea. On the western edge of Lynton, the 'Valley of Rocks' unfurls a broad majestic sweep of extraordinary lunar landscape, scooped out during the last Ice Age above overhanging cliffs, leaving jagged pinnacles of eroded limestone. Caves and clefts pierce the sheer rocks below.

Main: the funicular railway between Lynton and Lynmouth. Inset: Lynmouth in its steep-wooded gorge

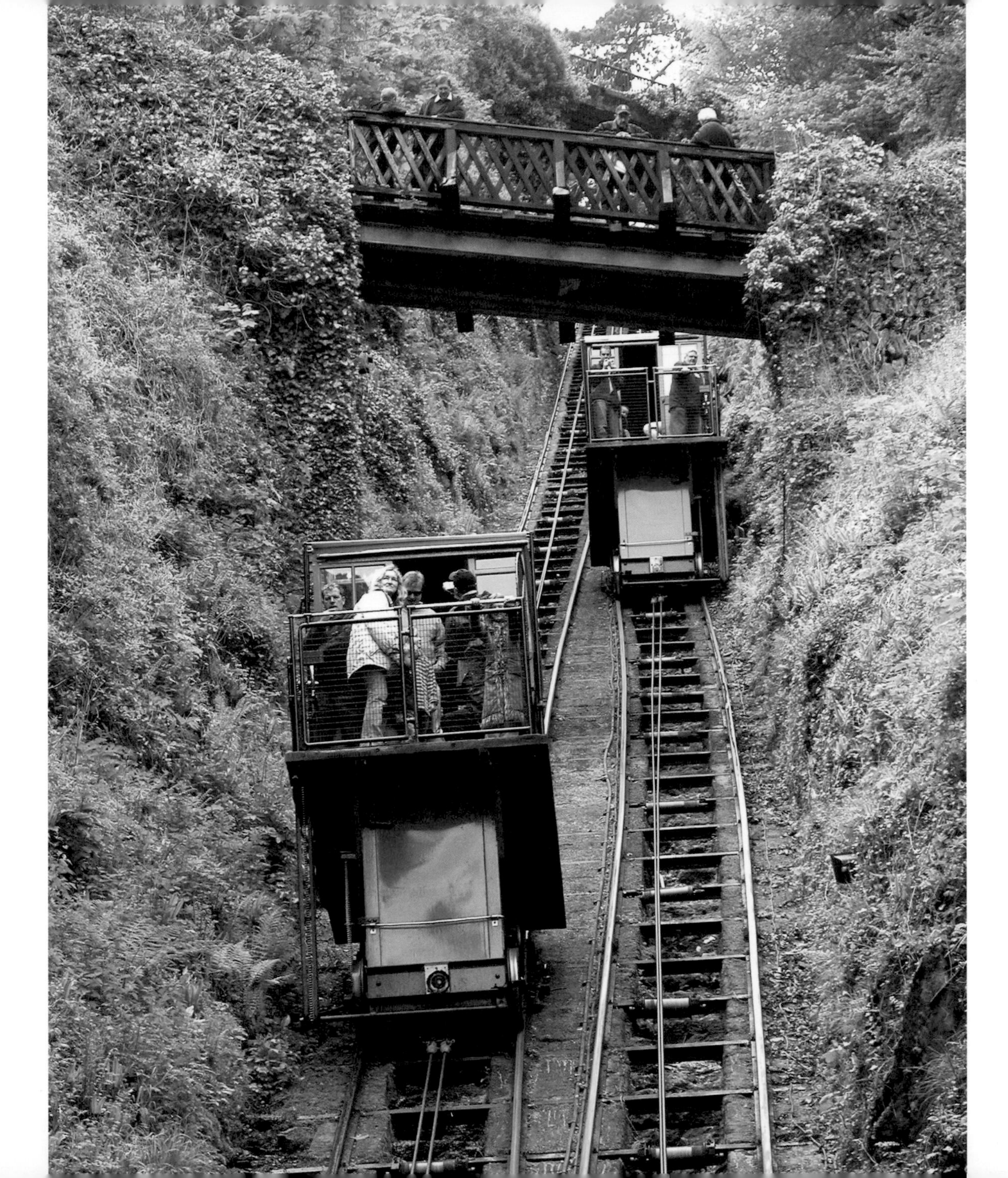

Mumbles, Glamorgan

Along Gower Road, Swansea's suburbs rise and fall across the hills whose iron ore and coal produced the city's wealth. I skirted Sketty and the darkly wooded Clyne Valley, dipping on down to the sea. In the gloaming, the lights shone on the water all around the eight miles of shoreline between the mouth of the Tawe and Mumbles Head, making the gigantic arc of Swansea Bay the most magical of all.

Mumbles is no more than an expanded village entwined with Oystermouth on an undulating promontory at this, the gentle end of Swansea. The green, wooded cliffs of Mumbles Hill rise above the shore road and the houses fit where they can and crowd behind the beach. On the furthest of Mumbles Head's strange rocky outcrops jutting out to sea, an eighteenth-century lighthouse still warns boats of sandbanks. It's a beautiful place. The great Norman stronghold of Oystermouth Castle, set high above the sea, was continually sacked and burnt by the justly furious Welsh, and then used as a quarry.

While picnicking on Mumbles Hill in 1872, the diarist Francis Kilvert wrote: 'The great fleet of oyster boats which had been dredging was coming in round the lighthouse point with every shade of white and amber sails gay in the afternoon sun as they ran each into her moorings under the shelter of the great harbour cliff.' Oysters were eaten by the Romans who had built a luxurious villa here beside the sea, and the oyster trade was lucrative until the late nineteenth century, when holidaymakers were considered more so.

In 1804 a group of local businessmen met in the Bush Inn on the High Street to discuss a means of conveying quarried materials from Mumbles to the docks at Swansea. As a result, a railroad was laid parallel with what is now the promenade, and on 25th March 1807 the first passenger railway carriage in the world was pulled by horse from the dunes at Swansea to Mumbles. The line was subsequently updated and was a great feature of local life until it was abruptly axed in 1960 by the demented powers that were.

Mumbles became renowned for its multitude of pubs, many of which have now closed. But The Antelope is still there – where Swansea's most famous son, Dylan Thomas, liked to drink when he was, as he put it, 'a bombastic adolescent provisional bohemian with a thick dash knotted artist's tie made out of his sister's scarf … and a cricket-shirt dyed bottle green; a gabbing, ambitious, mock-tough, pretentious young man.'

Main: the entrance to Mumbles Pier, built in 1898
Inset: gardens on the seafront

WELCOME TO
MUMBLES PIER
CROESO I PIER
MWMBWLS
PIER TOLL
PLEASE PAY HERE

Newquay, Cornwall

Approaching via the quiet residential suburbs, nothing warns you of the sudden splendour of Newquay's cliffs and beaches. This is the North Cornish coast at its best. Above Lusty Glaze Cove at the northern end of town, Glendorgal, once the seaside home of three generations of the Tangye family, stands proud on its windblown promontory. During the 1950s the author Nigel Tangye ran it as a hotel, restaurant and nightclub where, late in the evening, he sang Cole Porter songs. It was an exotic venue to find in Cornwall.

At the heart of things, the harbour wall and jetty which curl out from the sheer, sheltering cliffs were half built by Richard Lomax in 1832 and finished off by the extraordinarily ambitious Joseph Treffry of Place House in Fowey. He bought the harbour as a stepping stone for his tin and china clay which had to be transported from his mines and pits in Newlyn and St Dennis.

Treffry's death coincided with a dying trade and Newquay soon became the dream of Cornwall's greatest Victorian architect and entrepreneur, Silvanus Trevail, who wanted to create a Cornish Monte Carlo. He ear-marked the two best sites and today the Atlantic Hotel, designed to be seen from miles away, still towers in fortress fashion above the harbour, and looks towards the open sea. The gigantic red château-like Headlands Hotel is even more dramatic, standing alone on the isthmus of the Towan Head promontory. (Trevail, a depressive, shot himself in the lavatory of a train as it travelled though the tunnel near Bodmin Road.) The Church of St Michael, designed in 1909 by Sir Ninian Comper in the Cornish perpendicular style, is incredible.

Back from the sea there are frying smells, Methodist churches and boarding houses. Young people fill the streets leading down the hill to the beaches, rocky outcrops and caves. Surfers making their way to Fistral Beach through the golf course avoid flying balls by following the path which sinks below the bank and then rises up into the undulating dunes. Here there are large patches of single pink rugosa roses gone wild among the marram grass and succulent pink sea bindweed clinging to the sand. Below is Fistral, the finest surfing beach in the land, its long, even breakers booming in across the golden sand. There are gaggles of surfers all over the beach, groups of men playing beach cricket and girls listening to music in the sun.

Main: Fistral Beach with the Headlands Hotel above
Inset: surfers on Fistral Beach

Padstow, Cornwall

On rainy days, when Polzeath's surf is flat and the wind too slight for sailing at Rock, the regular holidaymakers, who have been coming to the estuary for generations, take the passenger ferry to Padstow as a diversion. At spring low tides the Camel estuary runs as narrow as a brook, and the ferry has to land at a nearby cove. A path leads along the cliff and past the war memorial to the horseshoe-shaped quay and the soft grey heart of town.

You can follow the harbour wall past slate-hung houses and souvenir shops, trippery fish-and-chip pubs, Abbey House, with its madonna lilies and sparkling granite steps, to reach the fish sheds beyond South Quay. Above them, the mountainous Metropole Hotel looks out of place – a reminder of the days when Padstow became the terminus of the Atlantic Coast Express, and the town's hopes were high. Dr Beeching closed the line, but when Rick Stein arrived in the 1970s Padstow's renaissance began – his restaurants have boosted the town immeasurably.

On May Day the houses are hung with green boughs and a hobby horse is followed through the streets to a haunting tune. St Petroc, Cornwall's best-loved saint, built his first monastery here in the sixth century, and the present fifteenth-century church stands on its remains above the steep hollow of the old town, with a thick half moon of trees around it.

Thread your way through the back streets to Fentonluna Lane which grows empty and quiet as it ascends the hill. Georgian and Victorian houses and cottages, their gardens stuffed with fuchsias and hydrangeas, line the way towards the gigantic ilex and beech trees and the peace of Prideaux Place at the top. This great lichen-smothered Elizabethan house, built of the local ragstone, looks out over castellated garden walls and turrets to a deer park which slopes down to the estuary. Under an ornamental bridge the way leads past field walls of wafer-thin slate set upright in tight-packed rows bursting with ferns and valerian. There is wild mint beside Trictroll, the footpath which takes you back to the cliff and leads above the estuary towards Tregirls Beach and the open sea.

Main: Padstow harbour
Inset: the Hobby Horse during the annual May Day festivities

Cafe
Fish and Chips

DRY DOCK

Penzance, Cornwall

After the Restoration Charles II made Penzance a coinage town where tin was weighed and taxed. By the early nineteenth century tin and fishing had made it a prosperous place and, coupled with its famously mild climate, Penzance became an obvious venue for seaside dalliance. Its incredible position in Mount's Bay, looking onto the fairytale castle on St Michael's Mount, was irresistible. Regency terraces and squares were built away from the fishing smells of the harbour, and palm trees thrived in their gardens.

Penzance has always been individual and exotic. In 1835 John Lavin, a native of the town and a keen mineralogist, built the Egyptian House on Chapel Street and kept his extensive mineral collection in the shop downstairs. It is made light of by architectural purists including Pevsner but, like the Brighton Pavilion, it remains an uplifting building in the true holiday spirit. The grandly magnificent Market House with its raised Ionic portico was built a year later and, together with a statue of Penzance's famous son, the chemist and inventor Humphry Davy, it commands the view down the seaward slope of Market Jew Street.

Not to be outdone, Samuel Pidwell built the Italianate Morrab House a few years later and planted a sub-tropical garden on the three-acre site which wound down from mid-town to the sea. In the 1880s the council took it over as a public park. A Boer War memorial was built in 1904, and shortly afterwards a bandstand was donated by a local coal merchant, Mr Bennet. The Penzance Military Band played at its opening ceremony.

In the 1970s the legendary beauty Jean Shrimpton bought the Abbey Hotel, painted it celestial blue and founded one of the best small hotels in England. It was way ahead of its time.

But it is art which pervades in Penzance today. One of the first-ever provincial art schools in the country was founded here in 1853 to encourage local working men to paint. It became a hive of artistic endeavour. Stanhope Forbes was a visiting lecturer (he later founded the School of Painting in nearby Newlyn – its painters became England's answer to the Impressionists). Peter Lanyon and Terry Frost attended the Penzance school and Bernard Leach pioneered its pottery classes. Today the town bristles with art galleries and houses Britain's largest collection of Newlyn School paintings at Penlee House.

Main: Penzance harbour with St Mary's Church
Inset: John Lavin's Egyptian House

Ryde, Isle of Wight

Ryde faces across the Solent towards Portsmouth's towered skyline. Three iron-clad forts (built in the 1860s in response to a possible French invasion) stand in the Solent looking like gigantic anchored vessels, as ferries and ocean liners sail between them, their wakes sending big waves onto Ryde's six miles of sandy shoreline. There are millions of pale pink shells scattered across patches of low-tide shingle on the way towards Appley Beach and its famous mock-medieval tower at the eastern end of the sands. A huge boating lake in the shape of a canoe, sheltered by shrubs and flowery banks, spreads out behind the 1920s pavilion (now part of a lavish twenty-two-lane bowling alley). It was once the site of a makeshift grave when England's largest warship, the *Royal George*, went down close by at Spithead in 1782. Many of the 900 drowned were washed ashore.

The workmanlike pier, completed in 1814 and later elongated, was one of the first in the country to be used as a landing stage for passenger steamers. Fifty years later a second pier was built alongside it to accommodate a horse-drawn tram, and a third sprang up in 1880 to carry a train.

The centre of Ryde on its steep hillside site is handsome, and its style distinctive. A grid plan of streets had been drawn up by the original landowner, and individual building plots were then sold or leased piecemeal during the first half of the nineteenth century. Houses were built according to their owners' idiosyncratic designs but conformed to a classical building code. On its airy heights Ryde feels a bit like Cheltenham with its white stucco villas, swelling bow windows and monkey puzzles growing in generous front gardens. The town hall resembles a Greek temple and Royal Victoria Arcade, off Union Street, must be the most elegant-looking shopping mall in the country.

Further down Union Street the Postcard Museum pays homage to the great saucy seaside postcard artist, Donald McGill. In 1953 the police raided five shops in Ryde, and McGill was later found guilty under the old Obscene Publications Act. One of the cards used in evidence against him depicted a girl approaching a bookmaker: 'I want to back the favourite. My sweetheart gave me a pound to do it both ways.'

Main: All Saints Church above the seafront. Inset: a saucy seaside postcard by Donald McGill

St Ives, Cornwall

On a walking tour in 1881 Virginia Woolf's father, Sir Leslie Stephen, came upon St Ives and was captivated. For the next fifteen summers he rented an early Victorian villa from the Great Western Railway Company and brought his family down from London to what he called 'the toenail of England'. Talland House looks out over Porthminster Beach and across the arc of St Ives Bay towards Godrevy Lighthouse. The St Ives branch line railway arrived from St Erth in 1877 bringing holidaymakers to the town, whose fishing trade was on the wane. The indelible memories of those holidays are threaded through much of Virginia Woolf's writing.

St Ives is romantic. It sits between two beaches, each giving onto a different aspect of the ocean. Today, looking down for the first time on the jumbled lichen-smothered slate roofs of the town which fall away to the curving sweeps of bay, it's hard not to echo Mrs Ramsay in *To the Lighthouse* – 'Oh, how beautiful!' St Ives never went out of fashion. Once the artists had claimed it as their own, marvelling at the clarity of its light and the sheer physical beauty of its setting, the world followed. Although artists like Sickert and Whistler had been coming here since the 1880s the town's connection with the avant garde began in the 1920s when Cedric Morris painted here, followed by Ben Nicholson and Christopher Wood. They brought the local Cornish artist Alfred Wallis's work into the limelight, and at the outbreak of war in 1939 Nicholson and his wife Barbara Hepworth decided to settle in the safety of St Ives, bringing their young family with them. An influential modernist group gradually evolved in their wake, including Terry Frost, Patrick Heron, Roger Hilton and John Wells.

The steep winding streets, alleys and tiny squares of whitewashed or slate-hung cottages around the harbour are packed with window boxes, hanging baskets, tourists and small art galleries. In among them, Trewyn Studio, within its lushly shady sculpture garden, remains an inspirational memorial to Barbara Hepworth, who left it to the town on her death. The new Tate Gallery fits elegantly and effortlessly into its setting above the white sands of Porthmeor Beach, where the surfers hang out and there are dark rocky outcrops among the grassy humps towards Clodgy Point.

Main: Porthmeor Beach, with the Tate St Ives on the right
Inset: a bronze sculpture by Barbara Hepworth

THE ROYAL VICTORIA HOTEL
ROYAL VICTORIA
CARVERY

St Leonards, Sussex

St Leonards is majestic. The well-to-do from Bexhill may not venture here, but it is their loss. The resort has now merged imperceptibly with Hastings (there was once space and a grand gateway between the two), but St Leonards remains a place apart. It is what Hove is to Brighton. The distant silhouette of Hastings's black burnt-out pier looks like a row of matchsticks when you see it from Marine Court – a clomping great Cunard Liner of an art deco building which feels as though it is about to weigh anchor and sail out to sea. (When it was completed in 1938 it was the tallest block of flats in the country and was nicknamed 'Monstrosity Mansions'. Today it is lauded.)

The romantic, steep terrain appealed to James Burton, a big London builder, who bought the farmland stretching for two-thirds of a mile along the coast. He was used to grand schemes, having worked with John Nash on Regent's Park, and his luxurious terraces and hotels along the promenade echo their style. The resort was carefully planned with a bath house, library, assembly rooms, a separate service area for tradespeople – the Mercatoria – and another for washerwomen, Lavatoria Square.

James's son, Decimus Burton, left his mark. Past his Greek-style assembly rooms on East Ascent, his lodged archway leads into St Leonards Gardens, a steep, wooded glen complete with a pond, from where you can glimpse the gothic Clock House in the trees. Beside the gardens, beyond flowerbeds of rosemary, catmint, phlomis and silvery mallows, the houses climbing Maze Hill are glorious – one half-timbered, another Tudor Regency. Past ilexes and yew at the very head of the glen, another Decimus gateway in the Tudor style sports a blue plaque on its eastern lodge: 'Sir Henry Rider Haggard, author, lived here 1918–1923.' The Uplands on these heights are the grandest semi-detached villas imaginable, in brownish stone with white stucco dressings and wonderful views to the sea below.

On 29th July 1944 at 11.40 pm a doodlebug which had been hit over the sea staggered for three miles and turned inland in the direction of Marine Court, where a big dance was being held. It deflected at the last moment and instead zipped up Undercliff and shattered St Leonards Church. God seems to have had a hand because no one was killed. The replacement church by Adrian Gilbert Scott, built in the 1950s, is fantastic, and contains stained-glass windows by Patrick Reyntiens, a dado rail of rippling stone waves, mosaics of local fish and a pulpit made from the prow of a boat from the Sea of Galilee.

Main: the Royal Victoria Hotel on the front. Inset: Marine Court

Salcombe, Devon

I came in winter down a deep, grass-middled lane as steep as a big dipper. Past Devon cattle the colour of the red earth on the hillside and past thatched cottages in Combe, the wooded valley begins to widen to the sea, and twentieth-century holiday houses and maritime pine trees appear, perched precariously above Splatcove Point. Salcombe visitors are well-heeled. Level with the sea, an expensive 'boutique' hotel looks as though it has been flown in from a gated community in South Carolina. Its terrace, hovering over the beautiful crescent of South Sands Bay, is packed with punters. Round the next wooded bend, North Sands, set with a little castle, curves to the foot of Cliff Road. As you climb up and up there are tantalising glimpses of classy 1920s houses half-hidden in fern-floored hanging woods. Then, way below, over the tree tops, is a ravishing view of the Kingsbridge estuary. The sea is aquamarine in January, while on the opposite bank the woods around Mill Bay, with its tiny golden beach, grow down to the water's edge. Even though they are leafless there is a luxuriant tropical softness about them.

This is not an estuary but a flooded valley or 'ria'. There is no single river but instead a myriad of small streams running down from farms and villages – Bowcombe, Oldaway, Frogmore, Batson, North Pool – into meandering inlets. Slate-roofed Salcombe clings to the scoop of the hill, with its church overlooking Batson Creek. There is a cluster of intimate streets and alleys packed with chic gift and clothes shops around the tarted-up harbour, and a few handsome houses and terraces from Salcombe's maritime and ship-building days.

Salcombe's idyllic setting gave rise to the inevitable lodging houses and small villas, and its life as an exclusive resort blossomed between the wars. The perfect waters were recognised by discerning yachtsmen, and today its holiday house prices are on a par with those of London. In summer the 'ria' is teeming with boats sailing over the Bar, a spit of sand just before the open sea. Locals say that Alfred Tennyson was inspired to write 'Crossing the Bar' after his visit to Salcombe.

Main: Salcombe (on the right), opposite East Portlemouth in the Kingsbridge estuary
Inset: Salcombe Boat Hire

Saltburn-by-the-Sea, Cleveland

Jane Gardam writes of 'a hard unhappiness' hovering over the Iron Coast (a stretch of Yorkshire coastline from the River Tees to Whitby), but there is also a feeling of great strength. The rocks on the edge of Skinningrove Beach are stained red with iron ore, the material which gave the area its *raison d'être*. From the nineteenth century onwards there were iron- and steelworks all around here, but they are now no more. The giant mothballed Corus factory stands back from the sea, and a notice stuck on the edge of a scrappy field reads 'Quality horses baught [*sic*] and sold'. Nowhere could be more different from the tamed South Coast.

If you walk northwards along the cliffs from Skinningrove and round the headland, Saltburn is set out before you, ordered and beautiful on its high cliff plateau, above one of the very best beaches in the country. Henry Pease, a fabulously rich Quaker whose family had founded Middlesbrough on iron and coal, built Saltburn as the result of a celestial vision. His widow described how 'seated on the hillside he had seen on the edge of the cliff a town arise and the quite unfrequented glen turn into a lovely garden.'

Within twenty years the main heart of the town had been built. Streets were named after jewels – Ruby Street, Garnet Street, Coral Street, Emerald Street, Diamond Street and Pearl Street – and the grandest of Italianesque stations sprang up. The world's first purpose-built railway hotel, the Zetland, boasted its own platform and looked towards the valley gardens. These were laid out with winding paths ribboning up the glen between pavilions and gazebos, and in 1869 the spectacular Halfpenny Bridge, spanning the whole gorge, a masterpiece of engineering, was completed for the sum of £7,000. (In 1974 it was deemed too expensive to repair and was blown up at a cost of £50,000.) But the thrilling lift built between the 120-foot-high cliff top and the pier remains an extraordinary legacy. There are only a handful of water-balanced cliff lifts like this in Britain.

The slow arc of shoreline stretches north, dipping down from Saltburn cliffs to the level marshes of Marske, and ending in the smoke-belching chimneys of Redcar. Surfers wait behind the rising rollers for the perfect wave.

There is nothing flimsy about Saltburn: not a hint of wedding-cake architecture. The respectable whitish brick streets, the solid, galumphing Victorian church, the large Edwardian villas on the edge of town, all display a down-to-earth solidity and a fierce sense of pride. The ironwork of the seafront balconies is robust, beautiful and peculiar to Saltburn. It reminds you that this area's foundries are still a force to be reckoned with.

Left: the Saltburn cliff lift

Scarborough, Yorkshire

Spend just one day in Scarborough and you slip into a good mood. Its natural setting is grand and spectacular, its flamboyant architecture uplifting. Added to that, Yorkshire people are friendlier than most. In the Crown Spa Hotel, perched high as an eagle's nest above South Bay, an old gentleman suddenly turned to his group of friends and said, 'I *am* having a grand time.' (I have never heard anyone in a London hotel expressing their happiness so overtly.) From up here you can see the generous bay curving slowly round in a long and perfect arc, and ending at the castle-topped headland which towers over the old harbour below.

In Scarborough you have a right to be proud. The British invented the seaside resort, and this is where it all began. In the 1620s Mrs Farrer discovered a mineral-water spring bubbling from the wooded cliffs above South Bay, and claimed that the waters possessed valuable medicinal properties. The locals swore by them, and gradually the fame of their curative powers spread. By the 1660s Doctor Wittie had published *Scarborough Spaw*, which advocated taking the waters for all ills, including killing worms.

He also recommended daily sea bathing. In no time at all the place was flooded with fashionable hypochondriacs. A spa house and dancing rooms were built, and the resort was born.

The town began to spread out from the thriving fishing harbour. In 1826 an elegant footbridge was built across the deep-cut valley to connect the main town to the graceful terraces, hotels and lodging houses which were mushrooming along the cliff top. On a rise above the centre of South Bay the Grand Hotel rose up triumphantly. Designed in the shape of a V for Victoria, its four domed towers represented the seasons, the 365 rooms the days of the year, the twelve floors the months. At the opening ball on 24th July 1867 in the Empress Ballroom, a full orchestra played a waltz especially composed for the occasion – and for a time the Grand was the premier hotel in Europe.

Though society abandoned it, Scarborough remains ever popular. In the morning you can take the steep zigzagging path from the Esplanade to the Clock Café, hovering above the sea. Then walk round the beach to the old town, which is a completely different place, with steep winding streets. You can dance down by the sea at a *thé dansant* and then watch a play in the stylish Fifties theatre where Alan Ayckbourn was artistic director for over thirty years.

Main: South Bay, with the Grand Hotel just in view on the left. Inset: the Clock Café

Sidmouth, Devon

If you approach Sidmouth on a fine day by the small road from the west and travel through the thick beech woods of Peak Hill, five hundred feet above the sea, the first sight of the town in the valley below will amaze you. It is the nearest thing to the Italian Riviera we possess. The hills behind rise higher than the red cliffs, which drop sheer to the sea at either end of the beautiful arch of shoreline. In winter Sidmouth is six degrees warmer than in London, and it claims to have less rainfall than any other South Coast resort.

Sidmouth was just a small fishing town when the speculative building of Fortfield Terrace began in 1790. Set back from the sea, the grand crescent, designed by the polish *émigré* Michael Novosielski, was never finished. In 1796 Emmanuel Lousada, an enterprising Jewish businessman who recognised the town's potential, built the very first *cottage orné*, Peak House, high on a plateau near the cliff's edge. Its style was the very latest thing and fed society's new passion for all things rustic and picturesque. Sidmouth became a discreet success story, with the brilliant publicist Mr Lousada at its helm. Bath was losing its hold as a fashionable watering place: Sidmouth, on the other hand, was burgeoning. Highly inventive flights of architectural fancy sprang up on the wooded slopes and above the shingle beach. In 1810 Lord Le Despenser built Knowle, a whimsical thatched 'cottage' of forty rooms, which became the most famous house in Sidmouth (it has since been altered beyond recognition).

In December 1819 the Duke and Duchess of Kent with their baby daughter, Princess Victoria, the future queen, took Woolbrook Cottage (now the Royal Glen Hotel). A cricket field was laid out near the middle of the town, and few places could rival Sidmouth. The Grand Duchess Helena of Russia rented one of the grand stucco houses on Fortfield Terrace in 1831 and is reputed to have brought a retinue of a hundred friends and servants in her wake.

The Sidmouth seaside style reached a peak of fancifulness when, some time around 1850, a Mr William Johnston bought Woodlands Cottage, tastefully gothicised by one of its former owners Lord Gwydir, and proceeded to lavish it with further ornamentations. He replaced the thatch with hexagonal slates and embellished the dormers with stone seaweed-patterned barge-boards painted sugar-pink, prepared in Italy and shipped to England. Sidmouth had gone about as far as it could go in architectural terms. Johnston's barge-boards were deemed vulgar by the aristocracy who still spent their summers there. In the end, the call of Nice and Monte Carlo was irresistible. They moved on, leaving the best collection of *cottages ornés* in the country behind them. Though Sidmouth continued to expand, it still retains a gentle, rarefied air.

Right: *cottages ornés* – Clifton Cottage, the Beacon and Rock Cottage by the shingle beach

Skegness, **Lincolnshire**

Beyond low-lying potato fields and isolated farms down dog-leg fenland lanes, Skegness sits safe on its mild rise above the sea. The churned-up sand shows buff through the choppy waves and an offshore windfarm wades across the grey horizon. Below soft sandbanks and patches of marram grass the beach stretches away for miles in each direction, curving imperceptibly to far-distant dunes.

The town has no pretensions, no claim to fame through royal visits, on which so many other English resorts have hung their hats in the past. It is a happy-go-lucky sort of place and was designed to be just that. Its parades and promenades along the shoreline sport the usual seaside attractions of funfair, fish-and-chip shops, amusement park, crazy golf, slot-machine arcades and gay displays of bedding plants – but Skegness was well thought-out in the first place and has a comfortable style of its own.

The Danes, who came here in the ninth century, left only the name. The small fishing village which lingered on was swallowed up when the new resort was laid out, all of a piece, in the mid nineteenth century by the local landowner, Lord Scarborough. He created an airy garden town whose broad, grass-verged avenues and boulevards leading down to the sea-front crossed tree-lined streets, forming a grid pattern.

There are well loved public gardens with band-stands and waterfalls, handsome Victorian houses, churches at focal points, classy villas with showy front gardens and a broad central street of red-brick shops with a fine celebratory clock tower at the end of it. It's the scale of Skegness that's so good.

Most of the Victorian pier was lost in the storm of 1978 – what is left just reaches the high-tide sea. A mile up the beach and hunkered down behind the dunes at Ingoldmells, the inspired entrepreneur Billy Butlin built his very first holiday camp in 1936, and introduced the famous Redcoats to the world. The camp, which slept a thousand, brought a wider fame to Skegness. The following year its capacity doubled, and today it can accommodate eight thousand people. If you walk south along the beach, as Tennyson did when he visited Skegness, you reach Gibraltar Point at the head of the Wash, where the seaward sands are treacherous and Brent geese migrate from Siberia in their thousands in winter.

Main: children riding donkeys on Skegness beach
Inset: the entrance to the promenade

Southend-on-Sea, Essex

The train from London strikes out through low, unsung Thameside Essex to muddier and marshier places. At Leigh-on-Sea there are cockle, mussel, whelk and jellied eel stalls on the mudflats between the train and the estuary. When you get out at Southend Station and start the short walk down the stretch of High Street towards the water's edge, and see the longest pier in the world venturing out into the North Sea, you feel you are on holiday – even if you are just taking an afternoon off from the metropolis. The change from the City's serious atmosphere to the frivolous gaiety of Southend is total. Whatever the season, the beautiful seafront is dedicated to pure pleasure.

It's hard to believe that gregarious Southend has its roots in a twelfth-century Cluniac priory in what was one of Essex's oldest villages, Prittlewell. From Priory Crescent a path leads across the park to the priory remains. A thriving community of oyster fishermen had grown up around its southern end, hence the name Southend. The town was slow to catch on compared to other seaside resorts like Margate and Brighton. Princess Caroline of Wales and her daughter Charlotte stayed here at the beginning of the nineteenth century and Southend became briefly fashionable – Regency terraces were built up on the esplanade above the sea, as well as a grand stucco hotel which gained the title 'Royal' after the princess's visit. However, by the 1820s the aristocracy had already deserted Southend and, although it retained a quieter, posher end around Thorpe Bay (still the smart place to live), it was the coming of the railway in the 1850s and the creation of Bank Holidays in 1871 that brought a different kind of success – hordes of day-trippers from London.

Southend acquired its clamorous cockle-stall reputation: London's East Enders could be by the seaside in under an hour. The hub of the resort, Marine Parade, gradually filled up with public houses. Slot machines, amusement arcades, bingo halls and funfairs abounded and the town spread outwards to Shoeburyness and Benfleet.

Despite the town's size and the fact that its biggest employer is H M Revenue and Customs, the seafront is still elegant and exciting. The pier stretches for nearly a mile and a half. In 1939 the Royal Navy took it over and it became an assembly point from which nearly 3,500 convoys sailed. A railway running along the promenade deck carried the sick and wounded in one direction and supplies in the other. You can still take the train to the end of the pier and sit, watching gigantic ships sail by.

Main: Southend Pier and Adventure Island Fun Park
Inset: a tub of whelks at a shellfish stall

SCARISBRICK HOTEL
Joint Carvery
AA
PITLOCHRY
PITLOCHRY

Southport, Lancashire

Southport is a sophisticated place. Facing out across an enormous inland lake which looks towards the Irish Sea, it trails along on the sandy edge of the low-lying Mosses, as they call them here. Once mudflats, saltmarsh, swamp and mere, spreading twenty miles inland, they were, like the eastern Fens and the Somerset levels, well drained with dykes and ditches by the Dutch.

At the end of the eighteenth century recherché villas and houses began to be built among the sandhills ('hawes', or 'meols' to Lancastrians). The local landowners, Madam Bold of Bold and her nephew Bold Fleetwood Hesketh, granted leases to speculators prohibiting the building of factories. The planning principles upon which the town developed over the next century made for a conspicuous absence of slums. There were never any telegraph or electricity poles in the town – all were buried from the start. Almost every house, however small, had a front and back garden. In effect, Southport was the first garden city in the country.

In 1825 an Act of Parliament was passed which included a provision that Lord Street, Southport's showpiece, should be 88 yards wide. Running one and a half miles parallel to the sea, with wide tree-shaded pavements, it makes you feel you are walking down some Continental boulevard. A handsome glass-topped wrought-iron verandah stretches out in front of the shops along Lord Street's west side. Coloured lights smother the trees at night and Victorian church spires, a campanile and a great obelisk rise up from leafy streets to the east. Napoleon III was said to have been so impressed by the scale of Lord Street when he visited Southport that his layout of nineteenth-century Paris may well have been influenced by it.

Although the six-mile-long stretch of sandy beach is only covered by the sea at spring tides (when it sweeps in at the speed of a galloping horse), this elegant resort has always been a desirable place to live. In Southport's poshest suburb, Birkdale, on the south side of town, Liverpool and Everton football players and their Wags live behind electronic gates in sumptuous red-brick Victorian villas with billiard-table front lawns mown in diagonal stripes. On the north side, Hesketh Park contains meteorological and astronomical observatories. The park's serpentine paths weave between high sandhills, clumps of Scots pines, flashy flowerbeds and out past a 'Tudor' lodge into quiet streets of Edwardian houses whose front gardens are full of almond blossom, amelanchier and clipped laurels.

Main: the red-brick Scarisbrick Hotel on Lord Street
Inset: the jetty

Southwold, Suffolk

Soaring above the lowland marshes, Blythburgh church tower acts as a beautiful beacon for the road to Southwold and the sea. Past strange salty lagoons beside the ribboning Blyth, Sole Bay Bowls Club hangs out its sign among comfortable bed-and-breakfast bungalows. There are rooks' nests at the top of wind-blown alders (the highest trees the birds can find so near the sea) and then the wide streets of Edwardian villas begin on the outskirts of this well-behaved town. It stands a little apart from other seaside resorts though its story is the same – once a thriving fishing port, it later promoted itself as a genteel watering place.

Southwold's gentility has lingered on, perhaps because the outlying salt marshes have curbed its sprawl. It is a handsome place with a grand flint flushworked church, a fat white lighthouse and the great Adnams brewery, a munificent presence in Southwold since the 1660s.

The 1900 pier, which by the end of the century was all but lost, was restored in 2001. It houses the wonderful 'Under the Pier Show', an arcade created by Tim Hunkin which includes the 'Autofrisk', a device to simulate the feeling of being frisked by inflated rubber gloves. The buses parked outside have lovely cream and green coachwork and beyond them, towards Easton Bavents, the beach strikes north under sandy cliff-like dunes and pastel-shaded beach huts.

Southwards, along the elevated promenade, Dutch-gabled boarding houses shield the old town, with its Georgian houses, elegant Crown hotel, tiny front gardens squashed behind railings, and the little red-brick house where George Orwell lived with his parents in the early 1930s (his sister ran the local tea shop). While he was here Orwell wrote *A Clergyman's Daughter*.

Apart from its beautiful beach huts and the Sailors' Reading Room, built in memory of Captain Charles Rayley in 1864 (a favourite haunt of the late W G Sebald), Southwold's peculiar glory is its Greens. The best one, which slopes down towards Town Marshes, is edged with Regency villas and cottages. Down on Ferry Road there are little wooden cottages crouching behind the line of dunes. Beyond them, Walberswick church rises above trees and an inlet set with sailing boats. There is a safety about Southwold which the writer Julie Myerson recognised when she remarked that the only things which have never changed throughout her life are her mother and Southwold.

Main: the South Green. Inset: the Sole Bay Inn and lighthouse

Swanage, Dorset

The Isle of Purbeck is a kingdom of its own. The villages around Swanage, like Langton and Worth Matravers, are full of quarry-men's cottages, all built of the same dove-grey Purbeck stone. They look as though they have grown from the landscape. Swanage, on the other hand, doesn't fit in at all. In 1935 the artist Paul Nash was appalled by its 'development' in what he described as 'perhaps the most beautiful natural site on the South Coast', lying between two great ridges of chalk downland. But to me, Swanage is a remarkable, quirky and often fine-looking place, and quarrying was always at its heart.

From the bold heights of Ballard Down, the jagged stacks of chalk-stone called Old Harry strike out to sea towards their counterparts, the Needles, visible on a clear day off the Isle of Wight. In the 1820s the local MP, William Morton Pitt, quick to spot the beauty of the bay, bought the manor house and some land, and began to develop Swanage as a watering place, albeit on a modest scale. But it was the town's great sons, John Mowlem (1788–1868) and his nephew and partner George Burt (1816–1894) who were to make the greatest mark. Mowlem had worked as a quarry-man in Swanage as a boy and made his fortune in the stone trade in London. Being childless, he asked his nephew Burt to join the firm, and the two men began to invest in Swanage. They rebuilt the roads and bridges and constructed a pier for the vast amounts of stone being shipped off the beaches from the three hundred acres of quarries above the town. Gas and waterworks sprang up as well as the Mowlem Institute, a reading room 'for the benefit and mutual improvement of the working classes'.

When London buildings were about to be demolished the Mowlem company had parts of them shipped to Swanage and resurrected – an obelisk from Ludgate Circus, a gothic clock tower from London Bridge, great Ionic columns from a grand house. When the company secured the contract for widening Cheapside, which involved pulling down the Mercers' Hall, Burt had its seventeenth-century façade stuck onto his new town hall. Further up the street his own house, a kind of Scottish baronial palace, contains bits of Hyde Park Corner, the Royal Exchange, Billingsgate, and Waterloo and Westminster bridges. Perhaps Burt's most eccentric addition to Swanage was his building of Durlston Castle, a tea room perched high above wooded cliffs with the forty-ton Portland stone Great Globe below.

Main: Swanage Beach, with the chalk cliffs of Ballard Down behind
Inset: George Burt's town hall

Tenby, Pembrokeshire

'You may travel the world over but you will find nothing more beautiful,' wrote Augustus John about his home town of Tenby in south-west Wales. 'It is so restful, so colourful and so unspoilt.' Tenby is impossible to top. However many tourists flood its streets and beaches in summer, it feels easy, settled and quietly assured.

Tenby's situation is fantastic, with the town crowding towards the bold rock promontory of Castle Hill, which is like the prow of a great liner sailing out to sea. Its lozenge-shaped grassy mound is crowned by a Norman keep and a towering statue of Prince Albert. Beyond them, at the furthest point, a dramatically placed bandstand hovers above the sea on a low cliff. Plaques on the wooden seats beside are engraved with visitors' resolutions: 'I will see more of my family' or 'I will pick up fifteen pieces of litter a day.' At the end of the point, St Catherine's Rock is cut off at high tide.

Castle Hill divides Tenby's magical and completely different waterfronts. The ancient quayside snakes around the huge sandy harbour of North Beach and looks towards the Gower Peninsula, while South Beach, backed by high cliffs, faces the Atlantic and seal-haunted Caldey Island, where the Cistercian monks sell scent made from gorse flowers. The oldest affiliated links course in Wales lies over the dunes at the western end of the resort.

Tenby is a walled town with roads still leading through the arches under the tower of South Gate. Inside, the medieval layout of narrow streets remains partly intact and feels utterly comfortable. It's a wonderful town to walk around, with sudden glimpses of the sea down steep, narrow alleys.

At the beginning of the nineteenth century, when Sir William Paxton, a Carmarthenshire nabob, had failed to be accepted as a parliamentary candidate, he decided instead to channel his energies into converting Tenby from a crumbling port into a thriving resort. He commissioned a great architect of the day, S P Cockerell, to build the public baths, above whose doorway a Greek inscription reads, 'the sea washes away all the ills of mankind'. Tall, reserved Georgian and Regency houses and terraces sprang up, set high above the beaches, following the undulating terrain. Today, painted in true rainbow colours, they look as good as seaside architecture can get.

Tenby was always posh. Its paths, looping around Castle Hill or down to South Beach, were solidly designed for Victorian nannies pushing large prams. In 1865 Queen Victoria's son, Prince Arthur, attended the opening of the Welsh memorial to his father on Castle Hill and stayed at the Royal Gatehouse Hotel (destroyed by fire in 2008). Tenby continued to be the favourite resort of the Welsh aristocracy well into the twentieth century.

Left: the sandy bay of North Beach

Torquay, Devon

'Torquay is a magic town built of high harbour walls and shining palaces beside the sea,' wrote Nevil Shute in *Lonely Road*. Today, you only have to blur your vision a little to obscure the odd 1960s block towering awkwardly among the elegant stucco housing, and the magic is still there. Down past the big hotels in Belgrave Road swags of coloured lights stretch between the lampposts all along the seafront, illuminating the Regina Hotel with its elaborate wrought-iron balconies, the Princess Theatre, the harbour full of sailing boats, a most exotic aquarium, and the jaunty Edwardian pavilion with green and white tiles, bandstands on its corners and fountains in its wake.

Torquay lies on one of the most beautiful stretches of the 'English Riviera', in the warm, balmy shelter of Torbay, between Hope's Nose and Berry Head, remnants of a great barrier reef. I walked down to Meadfoot Bay in the evening. The path zigzagged through kempt, palmy gardens from the grandest Regency crescent I ever saw, its long curve shining white above the sea. Precipitous, hanging woods clung to the hillside all around – Scots pine, ilex and oak sweeping dramatically from sky to shoreline – and the lights of Brixham began to shine across the bay.

Right: sub-tropical gardens in Abbey Park

It's the spectacular terrain, not the architecture, that is the dominant feature of the town. If you stand on Warren Road and look down towards the bay you will see that two thirds of the steep hills and canyon-like valleys of Torquay are taken up with great shoulders of rock or lush canopies of trees – planes, beeches, macrocarpas, cedars and palms. Striking between are steep, winding roads from which drives lead off to Italianate villas languishing behind gardens lush with hydrangeas and fuchsias. Twenty-three churches and chapels call locals and holidaymakers to God, and Victorian spires rise up against the hillsides.

The monks of Torre Abbey built the quay in the twelfth century, establishing the town's origins as a fishing hamlet. With the opening of the railway in 1848 Torquay saw the development of grand terraces and crescents, prompting Walter Savage Landor's comment that Torquay was full of 'smart, ugly houses, and rich, hot-looking people'. By the beginning of the twentieth century its respectability was so stifling that on visiting the town Rudyard Kipling exclaimed, 'I do desire to upset it by dancing through it with nothing on but my spectacles. Villas, clipped hedges and shaven lawns, fat ladies with respirators and obese landaus.'

Tynemouth, Northumberland

Everything about Northumberland is grand and bold. Even the Tyne seems to cut deeper through the heart of Newcastle than do rivers in other cities. At its mouth, the mighty northern headland of Pen Bal Crag juts out impregnable into the North Sea, surrounded on three sides by high cliffs. The ghosts of Iron Age men and Romans are here on its heights, and within ancient curtilage walls the sombre, dark gold ruins of Tynemouth Castle and Priory are silhouetted against the sky, romantic reminders that this was an important and powerful place. At the foot of the crag a massive stone pier which took forty years to build stretches out into the sea for a thousand yards, acting as a breakwater to the northern flank of the river mouth. Just south of the headland a statue of Admiral Collingwood faces out across his beloved Tyne. He stands on a monumental plinth designed by John Dobson, Northumberland's great Victorian architect.

Tynenouth is a cliff-top town, its old core of Front Street running in a wide boulevard down to the majestic headland. There are trees shading part of its grassy middle and good Georgian houses on either side. These include Mrs Halliday's boarding house where the writer Harriet Martineau stayed for five years during the 1840s in an effort to mend her health, and (on Huntington Place) the King's School, attended by Stan Laurel and Ridley Scott.

In the nineteenth century Tynemouth had a reputation for having the lowest death rate in the country. Speculators traded on this fact as well as on the beauty of its sandy beaches. They built a stalwart crescent of pale buff brick above King Edward's Bay, and one of the most glamorous railways stations in the country, all fanciful Victorian ironwork, glass, ferns and palms, like a gigantic conservatory (today, it's a brilliant venue for Tynemouth's famous weekend flea market). In the 1870s the Duke of Northumberland built a palace-like 'holiday house' for his wife looking down on the glorious beach of Long Sands. The Duchess didn't like it and within a few years it became the Grand Hotel – which it has been ever since. Below the hotel lies what was a wonderful 1909 seawater swimming pool, now converted into a forlorn-looking rock pool.

Back from Long Sands there are generously spaced terraces, the art deco-style Park Hotel and the aquarium, before Tynemouth melts into the former fishing village of Cullercoats at the far end of the beach. The American painter Winslow Homer stayed here in the early 1880s and a small school of artists followed in his wake.

Main: Long Sands beach looking towards Cullercoats
Inset: the ruins of Tynemouth Priory (with the lighthouse)

Ventnor, Isle of Wight

Ventnor's setting is spectacular. As you come over the wooded heights from Wroxall Downs the town falls sheer below you to the sea, its bottom-gear roads zigzagging in alarmingly steep bends past lush gardens behind buttressed walls. 'Here and there it clings and scrambles,' wrote Henry James, 'is propped up and terraced, like one of the bright-faced little towns that look down upon the Mediterranean.' In its Victorian heyday Ventnor was primarily a winter resort, its season lasting from October until June or July. The sheltered, south-facing town was said to be sunnier and warmer than anywhere else in the country, and when Sir James Clark (later Queen Victoria's doctor) published a treatise on the influence of climate in the prevention and cure of chronic disease, Ventnor's popularity soared.

At the time, about one in five adults died of consumption and, with invalids in mind, speculators moved in and built tall boarding-houses and hotels, stuck as though by glue among the rocks and ilexes on every available slope of the Undercliff. All afforded maximum exposure to the sun with double-decker verandahs. When the railway came to town a special 'Invalid Express' train ran regularly from Ryde. The most delicate patients were housed low down near the beach in the warmest place of all. As they grew stronger they were moved halfway up the town and finally to the very top, from where they could go for bracing walks on the downs. Only the well-off could afford Ventnor, but in 1869 a group of charitable organisations built the ten-block Royal National Hospital for Consumption and Diseases of the Chest above Steephill Cove, and gave hope to all. *Dum spiro spero* – 'While I breathe I hope' – was written over a door. The hospital was used for a hundred years and then demolished. The site is now smothered by the Ventnor Botanic garden.

Today, despite half the Victorian town being lost to bombing, landslip and redevelopment, Ventnor is still wonderful. A natural waterfall crashes down a mossy rockery under the 1930s Winter Gardens, and the old cinema is now a stylish Thirties-style apartment block. The town is also hauntingly romantic. In 1860 Turgenev lodged at Rock Cottage on Belgrave Road, where he began to write *Fathers and Children*. Evicted by his landlady for excessive smoking, he moved to a house on the esplanade to continue his work. Karl Marx convalesced here over the last two winters of his life, Alice and Edward Elgar honeymooned here in 1889 and a year later Mahatma Gandhi stayed in Sheltons Vegetarian Hotel. The poet Alfred Noyes was a resident for many years, and Swinburne, the hymner of the sea, is buried at adjoining Bonchurch in its deep cleft chine. In 1910 Thomas Hardy wrote 'A Singer Asleep' while sitting next to Swinburne's grave.

Right: Ventnor Beach with the houses in three tiers, originally built for convalescents, rising up behind

BLAKES
BEACH HUT DINER

Wells-next-the-Sea, Norfolk

Wells is at the heart of the low-lying stretch of North Norfolk coast between Cley and Brancaster. East of the town, the grey-green edges of the salt marshes melt into the North Sea. Muddy creeks and inlets wander among sand spits, eelgrass, samphire and sea lavender, and if you wait long enough, you might see marsh harriers, bitterns, redshanks, bearded tits, avocets, reed buntings or sedge warblers.

On the western side of the wide channel which connects Wells with the sea, a straight lane beside a miniature railway leads to the beach and the endless, shining low-tide sands. People look like ants in the distance, and away from the pretty group of stilt-high beach huts these vast expanses can feel utterly remote. In some places there are carpets of purple and orange shells which crush underfoot. You walk for what seems like a mile to reach the water, and shiver back across the rippled sand and round the wide lagoons to huddle in the dunes. At night, when the tide is high and a sand spit shaped like a crab's claw curls out from the beach, you might see sea trout swimming through the phosphorescence.

The Earls of Leicester of nearby Holkham Hall have long owned the land all around Wells – and it was they who, in the 1850s, distanced Wells from the sea by reclaiming the marshland west of the town and building the sea wall along the lane. In the 1930s they planted three miles of Scots and Maritime pine woods, stretching all along the back of the beach from Wells to near Burnham Overy Staithe. Today the woods are dark and eerie, and somewhere within their depths there is a log cabin which, I was told as a child, the Queen frequented. The woods also serve to hide Wells caravan park and the boating lake, known as Abraham's Bosom, once part of Wells's harbour.

Wells was once the most considerable port on the North Norfolk coast and was used by cargo ships until the late 1980s. The large brick granary looming over the harbour is a testament to those days. Today Wells is a seaside resort. There are pleasure boats among the fishing boats, stalls selling samphire, whelks, crabs and mussels, a family-run amusement arcade, the ancient Golden Fleece Inn and brilliant ship chandlers. Behind the quay there are whelk sheds, tiny yards and old maltings in among the grid of streets and 'lokes' (short, narrow lanes) of this handsome little town – all brick, flint, pantiles and the odd flash of a swooping Dutch gable. The Buttlands, a spacious green lined with lime trees and grand-ish nineteenth-century houses, sets itself apart (when the houses of Wells were officially numbered, the Buttlands refused to be).

Main: colourful beach huts at Wells
Inset: Golding's shop on Staithe Street

Weston-super-Mare, Somerset

Once you have passed the giant superstores and roundabouts spread-eagled across the Somerset marshland, Weston unfurls along the shore – the classic seaside resort. Its setting is superb and its dedication to the Victorian notion of seaside fun complete, even if some of their buildings are in jeopardy. The romantic Birnbeck Pier, for instance, designed by Eugenius Birch in 1867, steps out on delicately elegant ironwork legs across the water to a rocky island jutting out from the northern end of the bay. It was closed to the public in 1994 and its future remains uncertain. Meanwhile the Grand Pier never lost its formidable status. Even after a disastrous fire in 2008, it rose from the ashes to take its familiar place at centre stage in the middle of the promenade. It is bright, brash and confident, with three floors of games, rides and simulators. Its popularity undimmed, it is packed with people on any rainy winter's weekend. Miss England was being staged when I visited, and the sparkling pier-end restaurant was decked with black-and-white ostrich feathers.

The Welsh hills above Barry loom through the haze on the far, distant shore, and five miles out into the Bristol Channel the island of Steep Holm rises abruptly out of the brownish water like a gargantuan hump-backed whale. Knightstone, a small island in the lee of the bay joined to the promenade by a causeway, looks like a corner of Shanghai with its multi-turreted complex of luxury apartments crowding over the water. Weston's bay is sheltered by the wooded heights of Worlebury Hill, where the grandest Victorian villas, built of local pale-grey limestone and dressed with Bath stone, cling to the south-facing slopes. Brunel lived in the town with his family while he was overseeing the construction of his Great Western Railway, the arrival of which triggered Weston's property boom. The Somerset architect Hans Price (whose father-in-law was solicitor to Weston's major landowner) developed much of Victorian Weston and built some of its wackier buildings in all the styles he could muster – rusticated Tudor, Moorish, Flemish gothic and classical. The 1920s Winter Gardens – low, colonnaded and elegant – stretch along Royal Parade and there are several 1930s buildings intact, including the modernist Odeon cinema.

On Birnbeck Road the porches of a stucco terrace are topped by stone pineapples as big as dinosaurs' eggs, and on up the hill the road curves through a black rock cutting and into the hanging woods on Worlebury Hill. Sea-bent beech and oaks tower over the ivy floor, and winding steps climb up the combes, from where you can look back over the bay and down the streets of posh Weston to the glories of its front.

Right: the Grand Pier at night

GRAND PIER
2010

Weymouth, Dorset

A friend once described returning to England after a long time away: 'I have this dread about seeing England again. When you arrive at Dover or Heathrow after an absence it can look so dreary and depressing. Weymouth is by far the best approach. You see the town first like a Regency print in the distance, and as you get nearer there are small sailing boats, and you can just discern people walking along the esplanade. Everything is on a human scale. It's perfect England.'

Out on the front, Weymouth is glorious, with a long, graceful bay of the finest pale sand. It faces east, protected by high hills, its bay sheltered by the strange jutting wedge of Portland's peninsula. A smashing display of seaside terraces and hotels runs along the front – Georgian and Regency stucco and stone, alongside Victorian red brick. The jolly polychrome-brick Royal Hotel has pepper-pots topped by fishscale-tiled roofs. Bow-fronts and bow-windows abound, and back from the sea there are shelters which look like white wedding cakes, frilled with nineteenth-century ironwork. The old harbour is also full of stuccoed and bow-windowed houses, but they are smaller, more jumbled and painted different colours. There are quirky inns and ship chandlers in the winding streets behind.

Weymouth has played a star role in stirring periods of maritime history. It provided twenty ships for the Siege of Calais in 1345, six for Vice Admiral Drake's fleet in the Spanish Armada, and has given sanctuary to many a royal visitor: the pathetic Queen Margaret of Anjou sailed here in the hope of restoring her husband Henry VI to the throne in 1471. Most famously, Weymouth became George III's summer residence – on the front a fine Coade-stone statue commemorates him.

As a resort, the town was an early starter. Ralph Allen, who owned quarries around Bath, loved the place with a passion. He invited the Duke of Gloucester, and this touch of royalty was all the promoters needed. Weymouth took off, speculative builders moved in and, once it became frequented by the King at the end of the eighteenth century, there was no stopping it. There were balls and assembly rooms, and gaiety everywhere. According to a contemporary account from the 1790s: 'Many folk daily came into town to see His Majesty and the Court bathing in the sea water ... And some days the crowd could be so great on the sands that people are pushed into the water against their will.' The elegant 'Budmouth Regis' of Thomas Hardy's Wessex is still a place where anyone would want to be. At nearby Bowleaze Cove, an extraordinary 1930s Spanish-style hotel dominates the beach.

Main: Weymouth beach
Inset: Sand sculptures of *Alice in Wonderland* characters

LIVERPOOL VICTORIA
AMUSEMENTS
WHELKS JELLIED EELS
DOGS NOT ALLOWED ON BEACH BEYOND THIS POINT

Whitby, Yorkshire

Sitting in the cosy bustle of Elizabeth Botham and Sons' tea rooms (established 1865) on Whitby's West Side, beside towered plates of Yorkshire curd tarts, ginger cakes and lemon buns, I said to my waitress: 'This is as good as Betty's in Harrogate.' 'Madam,' she replied. 'It's better.' Whitby's pride is bursting, and justly so.

Between high hills, the town is set in a deep cleft where the River Esk widens towards the sea, secreting an upper harbour full of boats and clinking masts in the town's midst, and ending its twenty-mile journey in the lower harbour. Two lighthouses stand on the claw-shaped breakwaters to guide ships in between the treacherous cliffs. On Fish Quay there is a bandstand, a fish market and the white stucco Magpie Café, which serves the best fish and chips in the world.

Whitby's West Side is the younger side of town. A statue of Captain Cook commands the cliff top, looking out across the harbour where his ships *Endeavour*, *Resolution* and *Adventure* were built. There is an arch made of a whale's jaw bone which is testament to the town's history as a whaling port and to its famous son, William Scorseby, who landed 533 whales and invented the 'crow's nest'. (Whitby's street lamps used to be lit by a gas made from whale oil.) West Cliff, with Whitby Sands below, developed apace through the nineteenth century: elegant resort hotels and terraces looked to the sea, and streets of red-brick villas spread around Fishburn and Pannett parks. In the latter, the Whitby Museum displays the gruesome severed hand of a murderer, which was used by local burglars as a charm to send their victims into a deep sleep.

Whitby's famous visitor, Bram Stoker, described the town in *Dracula*, elaborating on the real wrecking of a Russian ship when only a dog survived, somehow scrambling ashore. Stoker made the dog head straight for St Mary's graveyard on the treacherous wind-blown eastern cliff top, as dramatic as any in the country. Connected to the West Side across a swing bridge, the old town huddles below the cliff. Cobbled Church Street leads slowly up the hill, past the old market house with its bulging Tuscan columns, past the Whitby Friendship Rowing Club, past ginnels sloping riverwards giving glimpses across the low-tide mud to Fish Quay, to shops selling crabs and navy-blue jerseys called 'ganseys', and to backyards full of washing, and on up the 199-step climb to St Mary's, 'the Sailors' Church'.

The view of Whitby from this high bluff is terrific, and so is the inside of the squat and ancient church, chock-a-block with monuments, beautiful box pews, a three-decker pulpit, galleries and stairs made by ship-builders – a moving testament to a sailors' community, to which the graveyard further testifies. Beyond the church, the gaunt Abbey ruins rise up – perhaps once the most spectacular and venerable holy site in the kingdom. The house beside the Abbey became a roofless shell after interminable storms – but there is now a museum behind its hauntingly beautiful Renaissance façade.

Right: looking along the River Esk to the ruined Abbey and St Mary's Church above the town

Acknowledgements

Thanks for their support and kindness to Clare Alexander, Peter Beacham, Susan Body, Cuddy Dalgetty, Lindsay Evans, Tim and Joy Farebrother, Robert Fox, Theresa Gibson, Justin Gowers, Maggi Hambling, Rosemary Hill, Barry Humphries, John Irvine, Tory Lawrence, Amabel Lindsay, Jane Orsmby-Gore, Josephine Pembroke, Judith Ponting, Sally Pyrah, Sarah Rees, David Roberts, Bertie Ross, Beverly Skull, Sue Spice, Cathy and Peregrine St Germans, Annabel Wightman, Ruth and Andrew Wilson and Henry Wyndham.

Undying thanks to Rupert Lycett Green and the brilliant team at *The Oldie*: Deborah Asher, Joe Buckley, Sonali Chapman, Claire Daly, Jeremy Lewis, and to James Pembroke and Richard Ingrams for their forbearance.

CANDIDA LYCETT GREEN

Select bibliography

SERIES AND GUIDES

The Buildings of England: The County Volumes, Pevsner Architectural Guides
The *Shell Guides* (various volumes)
Highways and Byways series (Macmillan)
AA Book of the Seaside (Drive Publications Ltd, 1972)
Reader's Digest Illustrated Guide to Britain's Coast (Drive Publications Ltd, 1984)
Through the Window: Paddington to Penzance (Great Western Railway, Ed. J. Burrow & Co., 1924)

BIBLIOGRAPHY

ADAMSON, SIMON H, *Seaside Piers* (Batsford, 1977)
BILLINGTON, PHIL, *Fabulous Fowey: The Visitor's Guide to Fowey and District* (Polperro Heritage Press, 2008)
BIRD, JAMES E, *The Story of Broadstairs and St. Peter's* (Lanes, 1974)
BRODIE, ALLAN and WINTER, GARY, *England's Seaside Resorts* (English Heritage, 2007)
CLIFTON-TAYLOR, ALEC, *Another Six English Towns* (BBC Books, 1984)
CLOUD, YVONNE, *Beside the Seaside* (John Lane The Bodley Head, 1934)
DRABBLE, MARGARET, *A Writer's Britain: Landscape in Literature* (Thames and Hudson, 1979)
DRAPER, CHRISTOPHER and LAWSON-REAY, JOHN, *Llandudno Through Time* (Amberley Publishing, 2010)
DU MAURIER, DAPHNE *Daphne Du Maurier's Cornwall: Her Pictorial Memoir* ed. Piers Dudgeon (Chichester Partnership, 1995)
ELBOROUGH, TRAVIS, *Wish You Were Here: England on Sea* (Sceptre, 2010)
EVANS, LINDSAY, *The Castles of Wales* (Constable, 1998)
EVERRITT, SYLVIA, *Southend Seaside Holiday* (Phillimore & Co, 1980)
GABB, GERALD, *The Story of the Village of Mumbles* (D Brown and Sons, 1986)
GARDAM, JANE, *The Iron Coast*, photographs by Peter Burton and Harland Walshaw (Sinclair-Stevenson, 1994)
GARDINER, JULIET, *The Thirties: An Intimate History* (HarperPress, 2010)
GENTLEMAN, DAVID, *David Gentleman's Coastline* (Weidenfeld & Nicolson, 1988)
GIROUARD, MARK, *The English Town* (Yale University Press, 1990)
GRIFFITHS, GRACE, *The Book of Dawlish* (Barracuda Books, 1984)
HERN, ANTHONY, *The Seaside Holiday* (The Cresset Press, 1967)
INGRAMS, RICHARD (Ed.), *England: An Anthology*, (HarperCollins, 1989)
KIME, WINSTON, *Skeggy! The Story of an East Coast Town* (Seashell books, 1969)
LELLO, JOHN, *Lyme Regis Past* (Lello Publishing, 1999)
LINDLEY, KENNETH, *Seaside Architecture* (Hugh Evelyn, 1973)
MANNING-SANDERS, RUTH, *Seaside England*, (Batsford, 1951)
MARSDEN, CHRISTOPHER, *The English at the Seaside* (Collins, 1947)
MUIR, RICHARD, *The Coastlines of Britain* (Macmillan, 1993)

MILDREN, JAMES: *The Cornish World of Daphne Du Maurier* (Bossiney Books, 1995)
NORMAN, JENNY; SCOTT, ANNE and CAINES, RICHARD, *The Good Beach Guide 1991* (Ebury Press, 1991)
NOYES, HUGH, *The Isle of Wight Bedside Anthology* (The Arundel Press, 1951)
PIPER, JOHN, *Buildings and Prospects* (The Architectural Press, 1948)
PRIDMORE, GEORGE, *Exmouth and Budleigh Salterton in Old Picture Postcards* (European Library, 1983)
PRING, SUE, *Glorious Gardens of Cornwall* (The Cornwall Gardens Trust, 1996)
SMITH, J R, *Southend Past: A Photographic Record of Southend-on-Sea 1865–1940* (Essex County Council, 1979)
SOPER, TONY, *A Natural History Guide to the Coast* (Peerage Books, 1989)
STEERS, J A, *A Picture Book of the Whole Coast of England & Wales* (Cambridge University Press, 1948)
THEROUX, PAUL, *The Kingdom by the Sea* (Hamish Hamilton, 1983)
VALE, EDMUND, *The Seas and Shores of England*, (Batsford, 1936)
WAITES, BRYAN, *The Bridlington Book* (Highgate Publications, 1988)
WILSON, DOUGLAS P, *Life of the Shore and Shallow Sea* (Ivor Nicholson and Watson, 1937)
WILSON, LAWRENCE, *Portrait of the Isle of Wight* (Robert Hale, 1965 and 1972)

Index by county

Picture credits

p.12 – Introduction © Kathy Archbold / Getty Images
p.13 – Introduction © Steve Smith / Fotolia
p.14 – Introduction© Paul Melling / Alamy
p.15 – Introduction © Rui Miguel da Costa Neves Saraiva / iStock
p.17 – Introduction © Lance Bellers / iStock
p.17 – Introduction © Grant Faint / Getty Images
p.19 – Aberdovey © Geoff Wilkinson / Alamy
p.20 – Aldeburgh main: © David Hunter / Photolibrary
p.21 – Aldeburgh inset: © Alan Blair / Photolibrary
p.23 – Alnmouth © Robert Harding / Photolibrary
p.24 – Bexhill-on-Sea main: © Candida Lycett Green
p.25 – Bexhill-on-Sea inset © Candida Lycett Green
p.26 – Blackpool inset, with thanks to the Blackpool Tower
p.27 – Blackpool main © Travelpix Ltd / Getty Images
p.28 – Bridlington © John Hill / Fotolibra
p.30 – Brighton main © Christer Fredriksson / Getty Images
p.30 – Brighton inset © Denis Waugh / Getty Images
p.33 – Broadstairs © John Haverson / Historic Kent
p.34 – Bude inset © Ian Francis / Alamy
p.35 – Bude main © Candida Lycett Green
p.36 – Budleigh Salterton main © PulpFoto / Alamy
p.37 – Budleigh Salterton inset © Candida Lycett Green
p.39 – Clevedon © English Heritage Photo Library
p.41 – Criccieth © Fotostock / Photolibrary
p.42 – Cromer inset © Michael Juno / Alamy
p.43 – Cromer main © Stephen Robson / Britain on View
p.44 – Dawlish © James Hughes / Alamy
p.46 – Deal main © Stan Green / Alamy
p.47 – Deal inset © PCL / Alamy
p.48 – Eastbourne main © Candida Lycett Green
p.49 – Eastbourne inset © Candida Lycett Green
p.51 – Falmouth © The Falmouth Hotel
p.52 – Filey inset © The Travel Library / Photolibrary
p.53 – Filey main © Loop Images / Photolibrary
p.54 – Fowey main © Adam Burton / Photolibrary
p.55 – Fowey inset © Michelle Simmons / www.iknow-uk.com
p.56 – Frinton-on-Sea inset © Neil Setchfield / Alamy
p.57 – Frinton-on-Sea main © Candida Lycett Green
p.58 – Grange-over-Sands main© David Poole / Fotolibra
p.59 – Grange-over-Sands inset © Tom Wainwright / www.yourguide2thelakedistrict.co.uk
p.60 – Hunstanton main © Jon Gibbs / The Travel Library / Photolibrary
p.61 – Hunstanton inset © Dave Porter / Photolibrary
p.63 – Ilfracombe © Philip Fenton / Photolibrary
p.64 – Llandudno main © Dave Newbould
p.65 – Llandudno inset © Getty Images
p.66 – Lyme Regis inset © Flora Bamford
p.67 – Lyme Regis main © Denise Drackett / Fotolibra
p.68 – Lynton and Lynmouth inset © International Photobank / Alamy
p.69 – Lynton and Lynmouth main © David Young / Fotolibra
p.70 – Mumbles inset © International Photobank / Alamy
p.71 – Mumbles main © Neil Setchfield / Alamy
p.72 – Newquay main © Gordon Sinclair / The Travel Library
p.73 – Newquay inset © Roy Lawe / Alamy
p.74 – Padstow inset © Paul Glendell / Photolibrary
p.75 – Padstow main © Stephen Hamer / Fotolibra

p.76 – Penzance main © Helen Dixon / Alamy
p.77 – Penzance inset © Robert Down / Fotolibra
p.78 – Ryde main © Patrick Eden / Alamy
p.79 – Ryde inset © Donald McGill / The Donald McGill Postcard Museum
p.80 – St Ives main © Lesley Pegrum / Fotolibra
p.81 – St Ives inset © John Warburton-Lee / Alamy
p.82 – St Leonards main © Candida Lycett Green
p.83 – St Leonards inset © Candida Lycett Green
p.84 – Salcombe main © Last Refuge / Getty Images
p.85 – Salcombe inset © Charles Bowman / Photolibrary
p.86 – Saltburn-by-the-Sea © Gordon Bell / iStock
p.88 – Scarborough inset © Alan Curtis / Alamy
p.89 – Scarborough main © Britain on View
p.90 – Sidmouth © Tony Evans
p.92 – Skegness main © ICP / Alamy
p.93 – Skegness inset © Mark Richardson / Alamy
p.94 – Southend main © Chris Lawrence / Alamy
p.95 – Southend inset © ImageState / Alamy
p.96 – Southport main © Jose Moya / Photolibrary
p.97 – Southport inset © Charles Bowman / Alamy
p.98 – Southwold inset © Rod Edwards / Alamy
p.99 – Southwold main © Picture Nation
p.100 – Swanage inset © Candida Lycett Green
p.101 – Swanage main © travelib environment / Alamy
p.102 – Tenby © Jon Arnold Images Ltd / Alamy
p.105 – Torquay © Kim Sayer / Getty
p.106 – Tynemouth inset © Graeme Peacock / Alamy
p.107 – Tynemouth main © Candida Lycett Green
p.109 – Ventnor © Dylan Garcia / Alamy
p.110 – Wells-next-the-Sea main © Gary Crucefix / Fotolibra
p.111 – Wells-next-the-Sea inset © John Hill / Fotolibra
p.113 – Weston-super-Mare © Tony Howell / tonyhowell.co.uk
p.114 – Weymouth inset © Carolyn Jenkins / Alamy
p.115 – Weymouth main © Peter Vallance / Fotolibra
p.117 – Whitby © Peter Reed / Fotolibra

Endpapers front and back – © John O'Connor, engraving